Prisoner or Patient

Prisoner
or
Patient

Lord Longford

CHAPMANS

Chapmans Publishers Ltd
141–143 Drury Lane
London WC2B 5TB

First published by Chapmans 1992

ISBN 1–85592–585–0

A CIP catalogue record for this book is available from the British Library

Photoset in Itek Baskerville by Ace Filmsetting Ltd,
Frome, Somerset

Printed and bound in Great Britain by
Butler & Tanner Ltd, Frome and London

To Elizabeth

Acknowledgements

I am immensely grateful to all who allowed me to interview them and to all others who helped me with this book.

Gwen Keeble was, as always, at my right hand throughout. I was much assisted also by Jenny Mackilligan, Barbara Winch, Kitty Chapman, Jane Davies, the team she inspires at 'Susan Hamilton' (Palace of Westminster), and Matthew Oliver.

Elizabeth also steadied my nerve as I plunged into these troubled waters.

Contents

Prologue: Anthony

Lord Longford: If you were dictator in this area, what would you do: (a) about the administration of the existing law? and (b) to reform the law?

Anthony: I think that we need to adopt a new approach to 'social crime'. That is, crimes which appear to be the result of addiction, mental illness, or plain inability to cope with the demands of civilised society. This would require us to look at the one thing around which all good detective stories revolve – that is, motive!

LL: Who is going to pronounce on motive?

A: I really don't know. I'm of the opinion that perhaps the psychiatrists should be asked to advise. We should examine motive, but I don't know how it can be done, or who is going to do it.

LL: Would you not agree that a number of people who break the law quite seriously must be sent to prison, and a number, presumably smaller, should be sent to hospital or something similar on grounds of mental disorder?

A: What is the good of imprisoning people?

LL: We are preventing total chaos.

A: Your Lordship is against crime and in favour of punishment?

LL: Against crime and in favour of punishment for some people.

A: At what point does one decide that a crime is so serious that only imprisonment will do?

LL: The judges have to decide.

A: But the judges don't seem particularly good at it. They send too many people to prison for too long in everybody's view, including senior judges. Perhaps then one of the solutions is to restrict the power of the judges to use imprisonment, except as a last resort.

LL: You have been before the courts many times. You have been to a mental hospital more than once. A psychiatric defence has sometimes been mounted for you. Do you consider that your conduct could have been better handled by the courts, either under the existing law or by a change in the law?

A: That's an interesting question. As you know, it's the problem of deciding that I have a 'treatable' illness. No one doubts that my behaviour is abnormal, but that alone wouldn't bring me before the courts; it's also criminal. No one has ever suggested that there's not something wrong. The problem that I present is one of having a mental disorder which is not yet treatable, and for that reason most of the time I have to be treated like a conventional repeating petty offender. It doesn't help at all, but what else can be done?

LL: Do you think some new kind of institution should be established for dealing with people like yourself – a special psychiatric unit in prison or a unit outside prison, presumably connected to a hospital, even where no treatability is expected?

A: Interesting question.

LL: Take acute schizophrenics: surely you don't think they should be sent to prison?

A: Nobody in their right mind would want to send a schizophrenic to prison, but of course it happens all the time, and one of the reasons that it happens is that hospitals will not provide beds.

LL: Do you agree, then, that we have a category [schizophrenics] who must be dealt with differently from the ordinary run of criminals?

A: The problem would seem to be that of responsibility. Is the schizophrenic committing the crime because of his schizophrenia? If so, then that ought to be a defence of sorts. However, if the crime is totally unrelated to the disease, do we then offer him the defence of his illness? I think that might turn out to be a jurisprudential nightmare.

LL: If the defence is accepted, what should be done with the schizophrenic concerned?

A: Anyone can answer that: he's entitled to be treated. The problem often is, should we treat him, even if he doesn't want to be treated? There are a large number of 'mentals' who actually wouldn't thank you at all for treating them.

LL: Do you mean that the choices are between treating him in prison; not treating him in prison; and transferring him to hospital?

A: I don't think there's such a thing at this time as treatment in prison. That's humbug. So we have the choice of not treating him in prison – which is what I say happens if he's said to get treatment in prison – or sending him to hospital. The problem is that the criteria for sending someone from prison to hospital are very limited and the mechanics are even more complicated. By and large, prison doctors don't believe in sending people to hospital for treatment if it can be avoided, and since they are the decision-makers, it's mostly in practice.

LL: When they get to hospital, do you think the treatment for such people is adequate?

A: I think we're not very good at treating most mental illnesses. The real question would seem to be whether it's right to put the schizophrenic in prison to deteriorate, or to send him to hospital, where he might at least be stopped from deteriorating, and might possibly get better. Clearly, hospital is the right choice.

        I can't emphasize strongly enough that the prison authorities shouldn't be allowed to say there's treatment in prison. If there is such a thing, then let us demand of them that they show us examples. I don't think they could.

LL: The advantage of hospital is that on the whole the staff are trained as nurses; the disadvantage is that mental patients don't know whether they will ever get out, and that is why they hate it.

        What form of treatment, if any, do you recommend in prison or elsewhere for a friend who is said to be suffering from personality disorder?

A: I want to think about that. I'm not at all sure there is such a thing as a 'personality disorder'.

Not for the first time, I was giving evidence as to character in a court of law on behalf of Anthony, who I had known for 17 years. Before and after I had become friendly with him, he had been to prison many times for short periods for minor offences – nothing remotely violent. On this occasion, Anthony had been convicted of accepting a stolen cheque for £50. Unfortunately, he was already serving a suspended sentence.

Counsel asked me, 'Can you give the court an impression of his character?' I was not as prepared as I should have been for such a general question, and after a pause replied, 'He has been very helpful to me in assisting other people on a number of occasions. He is capable of thinking beyond his own interests. He is affectionate and intelligent – and yet he goes and does these things.' I could have added that I had asked him more than once why he did these things, to which he had replied, 'If I could answer that question I would not do them.'

I should mention that Anthony's psychiatrist at his remand prison, Brixton, had put in a report that concluded that prison was not the answer to his case. A probation officer had written to the same effect. Admittedly, from these reports phrases like 'Walter Mitty' and 'manipulative' had emerged, which I sought to refute in my evidence. A well-known psychiatrist who had known Anthony for a number of years also threw his weight against the custodial sentence.

In the end, the judge said that the offence did not merit custody. In spite of his breach of the suspended sentence, Anthony was given a conditional discharge.

I tell this story because it highlights the difficulty of finding the right 'disposal' for someone who has committed many offences, but who also could be described as being to some degree mentally disordered. I had told the court that Anthony had been examined by many distinguished psychiatrists over the years, but they had seemed as puzzled by his case as anyone else. The label 'personality disorder' had been attached to him, but no one could suggest he ought to be packed off to hospital or prison. What, then, was the answer? I hope what follows will help to aid the search for the best, or the least unsatisfactory, conclusions.

Introduction

We punish people who break the law. That is a prerequisite of any civilized order. Ninety-nine percent of people [*sic*] are held generally responsible for what they do, including breaches of the law. However, when people are sick, we do not blame them. We do the best we can for them. Mental offenders are people who have broken the law and, at the same time, have been able to persuade us that they are suffering from some kind of mental affliction. Clearly this is a grey area, an overlapping area.

Those words were spoken by me in opening a debate in the House of Lords in November 1988 on 'mental offenders'. I still consider the words true in essentials. They begin a discussion which is carried on throughout this book and which is not likely to end in the foreseeable future.

(I have since adopted the phrase 'mentally disordered offender' as it is less likely to cause offence than 'mental offender'. The reader will come across references to the 'mentally ill', the 'mentally disturbed', the 'mentally vulnerable', and the 'abnormal offender', as well as to the 'mentally handicapped', as distinct from the 'mentally ill'.)

When we say that somebody is 'mentally disordered', we are making one of two statements about him or her, as compared with others who break the law. We may be excusing him or her wholly or partially from the moral responsibility which we attribute to normal law-breakers; or we may be announcing that he or she is capable of being treated by medical, that is to say psychiatric, methods.

The distinguishing factors in any individual case are capable of varied interpretations: Reginald and Ronald Kray were both convicted of murder many years ago. Reggie is still regarded as a criminal to be punished, and is in prison. Ronnie, after a long while in prison, is now considered a patient to be treated in hospital, and is in Broadmoor.

The ever-baffling question of mentally disordered offenders – how to distinguish them, how to grade them, how to deal with them – has been in my mind for many years. When I began to visit prisoners in Oxford in the late 1930s, one of my first 'clients' was a young arsonist. He was the same young man with the same problem, yet sometimes he was sent to the Oxford prison, and sometimes to the Littlemoor Mental Hospital. Where he ended up seemed to depend on the mood of the court.

Some years later, a dear friend of ours in Oxford 'went off her head', killed one of her children and tried to kill herself. She was rightly judged unfit to plead and sent off to Broadmoor. There she met a charming Polish man whom she married and with whom she lived happily afterwards. This must be described as a straightforward case.

Many years later again, a young man, Peter Thompson, now my friend of thirty years, in the course of a mental breakdown attacked three *au pair* girls and spent four years in Broadmoor as a consequence. Drawing on that experience, he wrote two books for which I provided the introductions. He has gone on to found and direct the Matthew Trust and in that and other ways to render immense services to the mentally afflicted. Since his time in Broadmoor I have made many visits to that hospital and, in recent years, to Ashworth (formerly Park Lane) special hospital near Liverpool.

But I am jumping ahead. In 1958 my book *The Causes of Crime*, based on a report for The Nuffield Foundation, was published. In the course of my inquiry, one of the expert psychiatric assessors, Dr Stafford Clark, made a strong distinction between medical and non-medical crime, which to me has always seemed to contain an ambiguity: is a crime to be regarded as 'medical' because full moral responsibility is lacking, or because in the opinion of doctors the person can be treated by medical means?

I regret having played no useful part in the debates on the Mental Health Act of 1983. Its impact on the fortunes of mentally disordered offenders is now regarded as controversial. In 1984 and again in 1988 I initiated debates on mentally disordered offenders. By that time the problem had come home to me, in particular the case of Ian Brady, convicted in 1966 for the Moors murders. A few years after his conviction, Home Office psychiatrists took the view, supported by the Home Secretary of the day, that Brady should be transferred to a special hospital. This was blocked by the Minister of Health, perhaps acting on advice from Broadmoor. After 20 years in prison, Brady was transferred to Park Lane special hospital, now Ashworth. The view held there by the doctors seems to be that this undeniably gifted man has been mentally ill since his teens.

To focus our thoughts, let us take a closer look at the debate on mentally disordered offenders of November 1988. The minister, the Earl of Dundee, replying, singled out helpfully what he called the key questions: Should more people who are suspected of having committed offences and who appear to be mentally disturbed be filtered out of the criminal justice system altogether, or at least, if in fact charged, be diverted into the health and social services?

Perhaps I should quote here from the *Independent* of 13 December 1991 concerning a Council of Europe report that described conditions in three English jails as amounting to 'inhuman and degrading treatment'.

As the Chief Inspector of Prisons, Judge Stephen Tumim, says . . . one of the most inhibiting factors is a 'lack of expectation that matters can ever improve'. Almost everyone has built up such strong defences against the grimness of conditions that they have become incapable of taking the initiative to improve matters – for themselves and for the inmates. . . . The visiting committee found no torture. But they were evidently shocked by what they saw as a 'pernicious combination' of overcrowding, inadequate activities for inmates, and poor sanitation and hygiene. We are all degraded by such disgusting and humiliating conditions in our prisons.

It is therefore more urgent than ever to consider the Earl of Dundee's second question: Is adequate provision being made within the prison system for mentally disturbed people or for their transfer elsewhere?

I
The Mentally Disordered Offender

Mentally Disordered Offenders and the Law

It seems necessary in a book such as this to describe briefly the
position of mentally disordered offenders under the existing law of
England and Wales. The treatment of mentally disordered offenders
is a joint product of the treatment of those who break the law and
of those who are held to be mentally disordered. I will concentrate
on the latter.

In 1939, for the first time, mental treatment provided voluntary
or temporary admission for some patients. By 1957, 75 percent of
all admissions to mental hospitals were voluntary, and in a few
hospitals the proportion was as high as 90 percent. The Mental
Health Act of 1959 broke new ground in decriminalizing mental
disorder and emphasizing the use of informal persuasive measures to
achieve effective psychiatric care. The most obvious result of this has
been a steady closure of the mental hospitals, the patients being
transferred either to smaller units, or to so-called 'care in the
community', which has not provided an equivalent volume of service
for mental patients.

The Mental Health Act of 1983 contained many of the basic
principles incorporated in the Mental Health Act 1959, with
amendments and additions intended to improve the civil rights and
other safeguards for the liberty of the mentally disordered. It does not
seem to me that mentally disordered offenders benefited from this
Act.

The crucial clause of the 1983 Act is 37(1) and (2)(a) whereby:

A court may by order authorize the admission of an offender to
and detention in such hospital as may be specified in the order or,
as the case may be, place him under guardianship of a local social
services authority, or of such other person approved by a local
social services authority as may be so specified.

The Act continues:

The court must be satisfied on the written or oral evidence of two
registered medical practitioners that the offender is suffering from

mental illness, psychopathic disorder, severe mental impairment
or mental impairment and that the mental disorder from which
the offender is suffering is of a nature or degree which makes it
appropriate for him to be detained in a hospital for medical
treatment and, in the case of psychopathic disorder or mental
impairment, that such treatment is likely to alleviate or prevent a
deterioration of his condition.

The terms used in the Act seem to satisfy no one. As Lord Justice
Lawton said earlier, 'mental and illness are ordinary words of the
English language. They have no particular medical or legal signifi-
cance, and should be construed in a way that ordinary sensible people
would construe them.' In this case, the lay person would have said,
'Well, the fellow is obviously mentally ill.'

This description of mental illness has been much derided but not
improved upon. In practice most psychiatrists include within the
category of mental illness schizophrenia, affective disorders, organic
disorders, and other syndromes which collectively may be termed
psychoses. 'Severe mental impairment' is what in common parlance
is called mental handicap.

But the phrase 'psychopathic disorder' has given rise to endless
controversy, which shows no sign of abating. The 1983 Act states that
if a psychopath is to be transferred from prison to hospital, such
treatment must be 'likely to alleviate or prevent a deterioration of the
condition'. In practice, this has often been interpreted to mean that
the psychopath, if he is to be transferred to hospital, must be curable.
This is not in fact what the Act says, but in the absence of adequate
facilities in the health service, psychiatrists have been given an excuse
for reading it that way.

Mentally disordered offenders can be remanded in prison for a
medical report; remanded in hospital for a medical report; or
remanded in hospital for treatment. The arrangements for hospital
orders are too elaborate to be set out here. A court may make a
restriction order when it decides to place the offender in hospital,
which means the patient cannot be given leave of absence from the
hospital, transferred to another hospital, or be discharged without the
consent of the Home Secretary. The result depends on four factors:
the law of the land; the efficiency of the arrangements resulting; the

wisdom of the individual making decisions about prisoners or patients; and the extent of the provision by central, regional, or local authorities of the resources required for the proper treatment of mental offenders.

GOVERNMENT ATTITUDES TO MENTALLY DISORDERED OFFENDERS

On 1 September 1990 a significant circular giving guidelines for dealing with mentally disordered offenders was issued by the Home Office and sent to the police courts, the probation service, the Department of Health, the health authorities and the Social Service Department.

The circular is mainly concerned with describing the present elaborate arrangements for dealing with those who break the law, but who can be identified as mentally disordered. The message, however, is clear: prison should be avoided wherever possible.

1. Chief Officers of police are asked to ensure that, taking account of the public interest, consideration is always given to alternatives to prosecuting mentally disordered persons.

2. Courts are asked to ensure that alternatives to custody are considered for all mentally disordered persons, including bail before sentence and that persons who are in need of medical treatment are not sent to prison.

3. Chief Probation Officers are asked to ensure that effective arrangements are established to provide courts with information and advice to enable them to make use of alternatives to imprisonment, in dealing with mentally disordered offenders.

4. Prison medical officers are asked to ensure that action is taken to arrange transfer to hospital under the provisions of Section 48 of the Mental Health Act 1983 in respect of any mentally ill or severely mentally impaired person remanded in custody who appears to require treatment in hospital.

The circular encloses a number of appendices, some of them describing attempts already being made to give effect to these excellent aspirations. Appendix D is entitled 'Health Service Provision for the Treatment and Care of Mentally Disordered Prisoners'; subheadings include: 'Forensic Psychiatric Service', 'Local Psychiatric Services', 'Regional Secure Units and Special Hospitals'. The responsibilities of local authority Social Services Departments are also indicated. I have not met anyone with any claims to expertise who considered that these provisions, so impressive on paper, provide a satisfactory treatment in practice for mental offenders. Hence the present book.

The government circular stresses the need to transfer mentally disordered prisoners to hospital. Who wills the end, however, must will the means. Let me give an example: The Psychiatric Liaison Scheme to Clerkenwell and Hampstead Magistrates' Court (sitting at Clerkenwell) in London was established in 1990 on the initiative of the local Probation Service, following concern about the difficulty of obtaining psychiatric reports with reasonable speed. Prisoners in need of assessment are remanded until the day of the psychiatrists' visit. The psychiatrists obtain information about each person from general practitioners' and probation files, defence solicitors, hospitals, the social services and relatives. Reports are given orally in court. Efforts are made to ensure that all those put 'on section' are admitted to hospital direct from the court.

The great merit of the scheme is that it shortens the period which mentally disordered patients spend between their arrest and their arrival in hospital. Normally, prisoners are remanded to Brixton prison where the arrangements for them to see psychiatrists seem to be elaborate and prolonged, whereas under the Clerkenwell plan the stay in prison on the way to hospital is reduced by an average of two weeks. Funding, as so often, is limited. Certainly when I visited the Magistrates' Court the conditions were remarkably cramped. At the present time the psychiatrists' fees are paid out of 'witnesses' expenses'. I cannot resist the conclusion of the Chief Clerk and the psychiatrists that the benefits of adequate funding would be 'out of proportion to the relatively small sum involved'. There is, I gather, only one other scheme of this kind functioning at the present time. The services of psychiatrists should be available to every court, a number of courts being covered by a single service. But nothing will happen unless the Home Office, who have indicated their approval, back up their words with funding.

THE BUTLER REPORT OF THE COMMITTEE ON MENTALLY ABNORMAL OFFENDERS

Modern thinking on mentally disordered offenders may be said to start with the report of the committee presided over by Lord Butler, which was published in October 1975. In historical perspective, an interim report published in April 1974 was of more lasting importance. This report recommended as a matter of urgency the provision of secure hospital units in each regional authority area:

> To avoid local financial difficulties it is proposed that this provision should be financed by direct allocation of central government funds to the regional health authorities . . . The units are required for those mentally disordered persons, offenders and non-offenders alike, who do not require the degree of security offered by the Special Hospitals, but who none-the-less are not suitable for treatment under the open conditions obtaining in local psychiatric hospitals.

At the time of writing this book, 15 years later, only 600 places of this kind have been provided instead of the 2,000 recommended by the Butler Committee.

In their final report the Committee mentioned certain guiding principles they were following:

1. Everything practical should be done to ensure that the occurrence of mental disorder is recorded at the appropriate stage of the legal process.
2. That there should be the greatest possible flexibility in disposal.
3. The arrangements should safeguard the mentally disordered person, whom it would be unjust to try.
4. That the mentally disordered offender should be placed in the

> treatment situation which is best for him, consistent with the requirements of public safety.
>
> 5. That treatment should be made available as soon as possible.

While these objectives must seem to be acceptable to all, the fourth one causes one to pause for a moment. As long ago as 1961 in my book *The Idea of Punishment* I suggested there were four elements in a just punishment: deterrence, retribution, prevention, and reform (reparation should figure much more prominently in future). The Butler Committee was saying that two of these, deterrence and retribution, should not apply to mentally disordered offenders; we should be relying on prevention (detention of prisoners in the interests of their own and the public security), and reform (compare the situation today in the special hospitals).

The other main recommendations of the Butler Committee relate to the concept of dangerousness, proposing a new form of indeterminate sentence from which release would be entirely dependent on whether or not the individual was considered dangerous:

> The sentence should be for offenders who are dangerous, who present a history of mental disorder which cannot be dealt with under the Mental Health Act, and for whom a life sentence is not appropriate. It would be subject to statutory review at regular (two-yearly) intervals. On release, the offender should be under police supervision, again subject to statutory review.

It is difficult to say whether the idea of 'dangerousness' is accepted in legislation at the present time. In the Criminal Justice Act 1991 it lurks below the surface. And in granting or refusing parole, it no doubt figures importantly in calculations. Some of those who like myself were concerned with the original propagation of the parole idea consider dangerousness to have been played down too much in recent years and deterrence and retribution played up too much accordingly.

Bluglass and Bowden's *Forensic Psychiatry* contains two chapters concerned with the idea of dangerousness. Psychiatrists appear to be divided as to how far they are able to decide whether a person is likely to be dangerous in the future. One has made elaborate suggestions as to how the concept of dangerousness may be applied without imperilling human liberties:

1. We might exclude many property offences from our consideration;
2. Previous similar conduct would help to establish whether or not aberration existed;
3. A further rule should operate in the offender's favour – if the incentives for his initial offending had ceased to exist;
4. Measures other than detention should be used if possible;
5. The conditions of detention on the grounds of dangerousness should be as humane and tolerable as possible.

In general, it would seem that the concept of dangerousness, like the provision of secure hospital units, has not made much progress since the Butler Committee Report of 1975.

II
The Judicial Approach

The Sentence of the Court

'Provoked Wife Loses Murder Plea'
'Killer Goes Free'
'Mother's Robbery Sentence Lifted'

These three recent headlines from the *Guardian* illustrate the problem facing our judges. In the first case, a woman who had stabbed her alcoholic and violent husband to death lost her appeal against conviction for murder, despite the fact that she suffered from a personality disorder and had attempted suicide on a number of occasions. In the second case, a woman who admitted to stabbing to death a bullying thug after he attacked her friend was put on probation for three years. She is receiving medication for premenstrual tension. In the third case, a woman who had robbed seven building societies was freed from a four-year prison sentence by the Court of Appeal. The judge decided she was undoubtedly unwell and in urgent need of treatment.

In the two interviews that follow, it will be noticed that Mr Justice (Sir Robin) Auld and Lord Justice (Sir Patrick) O'Connor pay much attention to the guidelines (*Sentencing – Guideline Cases*) issued by the Appeal Court. But for magistrates, the key document with regard to sentencing is *The Sentence of the Court*. It should be helpful to the reader to be aware of the passages concerned with mentally disordered offenders.

> It will seldom be appropriate or effective to give a mentally disordered offender a custodial sentence. In particular such action should not be regarded as a means of securing for the offender such psychiatric treatment as he needs.

The Sentence of the Court begins by stating that 'most of the special powers required for dealing with mentally disordered offenders are to be found within the meaning of the Mental Health Act 1983.' It goes on to point out that many others whose condition does not fall within the scope of the Act are nevertheless suffering from some form of mental disturbance or disorder.

It continues:

> When the use of powers under the Mental Health Act 1983 is not appropriate, it is nevertheless right to take account of the defendant's mental condition in deciding what disposal is appropriate. The Court has available to it a wide range of non-custodial options for a comparatively minor offence. Absolute or conditional discharge may well be sufficient sanction. [This was apparently the attitude of the court in the case of Anthony, described at the beginning of this book.]

The handbook goes on to mention probation and the power to make a probation order, including the requirement that the probationer submits to psychiatric treatment. What is left somewhat nebulous is the fate of those who do not fall within the scope of the 1983 Act, but whose offence is too serious for them to be left in the community.

The handbook is gloomy about the psychiatric service that is at present rendered in prison:

> The Prison Medical Service seeks to do what they can to help mentally disordered people who, as a last resort, the court has sent to prison. But only a very small number of prison establishments have developed the specialized facilities offering a range of therapies in special cases. In general terms, however, the fact of imprisonment and the overcrowding and conditions prevailing in prisons are not conducive to a healing environment. It would be wrong to proceed on the basis that such facilities as exist in the prison service are comparable to those in psychiatric hospitals in the community.

Mr Justice (Sir Robin) Auld
High Court Judge, Queen's Bench Division

I had sent Mr Justice Auld various questions before our meeting, which helped him no doubt to set out his views. I began by asking him about *Sentencing – Guideline Cases*, which I understood played a large part in his sentencing decisions. He replied:

> These are simply extracts from published law reports of certain cases in which the Court of Appeal [Criminal Division] has set out to give general guidance for specific types of offences. Not every type of offence is covered by a guideline; for example, there is no guideline for theft or burglary. They are, as their name indicates, only guidelines, not rigid sentencing directions. Their purpose is to encourage that elusive concept consistency in sentencing, bearing in mind always the particular circumstances of each case.

He felt that a number of elements are involved in 'the just sentence':

> . . . sentencing, depending upon the type of offence and the circumstances of the offender and the victim, may involve some or all of the following purposes: retribution or punishment, deterrence, prevention, reform of the offender and reparation. With the overcrowded and badly resourced prisons that we have, most judges, and, I believe, the prison service, do not rate prison highly as a means of reforming the offender.

Is this attitude more or less helpful to prisoners? On the one hand, it would make judges reluctant to send someone to prison 'to improve his character'. On the other hand, the abandonment of the rehabilitative ideal in prisons could have, and I believe has had, damaging effects on prison life. Mr Justice Auld went on to say that the:

> . . . notion of blame or wickedness, which goes to one of the purposes of sentencing, punishment, plays an important part in the sentencing decision. The guidelines, where there are such, and the

> digest of reported sentences for each type of offence . . . give a judge a rough scale to which he can give effect in his assessment of blame, i.e., the need for punishment, along with the other purposes of sentencing . . .

There followed a thought-provoking, if controversial, explanation of why the judges in this country send more people to prison than they would wish to:

> The instincts of the judiciary are against imprisonment if they are satisfied that some alternative has a reasonable chance of success. The problem is that the judiciary has been faced for some years with a probation service many of whom do not view their role as providing a rigorous alternative in the community, but regard offenders put in their charge as 'their clients'. The service is also under-funded, so that even where probation officers are minded to adopt a more active training and 'policing' role, they have not the resources to do it. Neither of these problems will be solved by the 1991 Criminal Justice Act. Many in the probation service are hostile to the increased role in community-based sentencing envisaged for them by the legislation, and the additional resources committed to it by the government are likely to be inadequate.

We turned to my immediate topic, mentally disordered offenders, and he answered my question regarding the apportionment of blame incisively: 'Whether a judge is concerned with blame when sentencing a mentally disordered offender depends upon the exercise he is being asked to do.'

Mr Justice Auld distinguished three classes of case:

> If he is being invited to make a hospital order under Section 37 of the Mental Health Act 1983, he will normally exercise his discretion to do so if he is satisfied on the evidence of two suitably qualified doctors that the offender is mentally ill or disordered as defined in that Section. He will impose a restriction order under Section 41 if on the medical evidence it is necessary for the protection of the public. There is no question of blame requiring punishment in this sentencing exercise.

Where a judge has to sentence a person found guilty of manslaughter by reason of diminished responsibility, he is required by a decision of the Court of Appeal [Criminal Division], where a hospital order is not recommended, to fix a sentence having regard to his assessment of the degree of the offender's responsibility for his act and his view as to the period of time, if any, for which the offender will be a danger to the public. This exercise . . . necessarily involves some assessment by the judge, assisted by the medical and any other evidence put before him, of the offender's blameworthiness.

The Judge, it will be noted, draws a crucial distinction between the first and second categories. In the first case there is no question of blame; in the second the judge has the task of assessing the offender's blameworthiness. What Mr Justice Auld said next was of special interest.

The most difficult sentencing decision for a judge where there is some mental element involved that falls short of a mental illness or disorder justifying the making of a hospital order under the Mental Health Act 1983 is in cases involving sexual offences or offences triggered by alcohol or drug abuse. Here a judge has to balance the purposes of punishment [blame] and short-term prevention on the one hand against the possibility of achieving long-term prevention by treatment [reform] of the offender as a condition of probation.

What Mr Justice Auld said next brings us back to the fact that sentencing is a matter of balancing a number of separate factors:

The weight that he [the judge] gives to the possibility of reform by treatment will necessarily depend upon the strength of the medical evidence put before him. Even if he is satisfied that there is a high probability of success, the crime may be so grave [the offender's blame so great] and the danger to the public so great if he should re-offend that punishment and prevention will prevail.

Lord Justice (Sir Patrick) O'Connor
Former Lord Justice of Appeal

Lord Longford:	Generally speaking, would you say that the level of sentencing in this country is determined by the standards set in the Appeal Court?
Sir Patrick:	Yes – in the Appeal Court for serious crimes, but magistrates who are dealing with a whole raft of offences have guidelines from sentencing seminars as well as from the Crown Court sitting in its appellate capacity. Magistrates' sentences do not come to the Court of Appeal. There are hundreds of offences, for example, connected with motoring. These sentences are regulated by sentencing seminars for justices, sometimes by justices being addressed by senior judges on circuit, or occasionally by the Lord Chief Justice.
LL:	You do not conceive yourself as being ultimately responsible for magistrates' sentences?
SP:	They never reach us.
LL:	On the question of the mentally disordered, I notice in the official book on sentencing there is no heading devoted to mentally disordered cases. Does that suggest that the Appeal Court have not brought their minds to bear on the subject?
SP:	No. It is endemic in setting sentences to look at the mental capacity of the defendant. For example, what sentence should be passed on someone who has no defence to the actual offence? Is it a case for prison, or a hospital order, or for probation coupled with an order for psychiatric treatment? That is all decided by the judge on medical evidence, which is produced at the sentencing session. It may have been very early on in the case, but usually after a person or defendant has been found guilty by the jury. The sentence exercise may call

for a social enquiry by the court, and for medical reports if there is a hint of mental disturbance, and the judge may remand until he has received such medical reports.

LL: The judge has to decide whether the medical evidence should prevail?

SP: Yes. If there is conflicting medical evidence, he or she has to choose. However, once a person is tried for murder and is found guilty, then the judge has no discretion.

LL: Generally speaking, when passing sentence, what allowance does the judge make for psychiatric factors?

SP: The difficulty comes with considering the question of danger to the public. During the late 1960s or early 1970s it became fashionable not to send people to prison, but to make hospital orders with or without restrictions as to time. Doctors, however, did not want to accept people who had committed serious crimes in their hospitals, or those whom they could not cure. If doctors thought that a defendant was possibly suffering from a mental condition not susceptible to treatment, they would say there was nothing the matter with the person. Medical evidence in court must be given by two doctors; the jury does not come into it. The jury is only concerned as to whether the defendant is guilty, and it is no defence to say he is mentally disturbed.

LL: If the medical advice is confirmed, should the defendant not plead but be sent to hospital? But if it is not confirmed, would the judge have to put it to the jury?

SP: The jury's only concern is if before the trial the defence is that he is insane and not fit to be tried. If that is the case, the judge will empanel a jury to try that issue. Evidence has to be produced for the judge to show he should do so.

LL: Assuming that the man is tried and found guilty and the question of mitigation is put, that is an important issue.

If, for example, it had been alleged in the Guinness trial that Ernest Saunders was suffering from pre-senile dementia, would that have been established as a mitigating factor?

SP: Does the evidence call for a prison sentence? If it does, it has got to be prison. The length of the sentence will to some extent be affected by the personal circumstances of the defendant.

LL: What is the real principle at issue here – compassion?

SP: The principle must be to produce a just sentence for the convicted individual. Some people will suffer confinement in prison more harshly than others. Judges have always borne this in mind, and certainly in the Appeal Court you have to bear in mind when dealing with somebody who is a 'grass' that incarceration will be much more severe.

LL: Do you pay attention to evidence of character? I gave evidence as to character recently on behalf of a defendant involved in a serious drug importation conspiracy. He was given 25 years, plus another five if he failed to pay an additional heavy fine. A very severe sentence, despite the fact that he is a man in his mid-50s, suffering from asthma. In terms of a plea for mitigation – would it count that he was in bad health?

SP: Not really. It was indeed a severe sentence, but it must have been a large-scale importation of a hard drug like cocaine. For wholesale importation of hard drugs it was certainly not out of line.

LL: Does his medical condition affect his sentence?

SP: Generally speaking, no. But in an extreme case it may, and as you know, the Home Office can release people in the last few weeks if they are obviously dying. But I don't know if the judge is going to concern himself with that, unless it is immediate. I can't remember what the medical evidence was in the case of Ernest Saunders. You won't get a perfect spectrum in any event, because judges are human.

LL: Is it a question of the amount of suffering the person is going to undergo in prison?

SP: In a relevant case, yes, it is a factor.

LL: How far do judges, consciously or unconsciously, explicitly or implicitly, allow public opinion to affect their decisions?

SP: I don't think they are much influenced by it. But obviously, as a human being, the nature of the offence is a factor. The public may feel abhorrence for a particular form of activity; the judge, as a member of the public himself, cannot divorce himself from it. The very nature of the offence will often be reflected in the sentence. The revulsion the public may feel will be felt by the judge as well. I do not see that it is avoidable.

LL: I don't think that others' feelings should govern the sentence.

SP: In murder cases, the judge writes a note to the Home Secretary and may or may not mention the nature of the offence or give the retribution limits. He will say how long the offender should serve, and when the parole board considers the case, the Lord Chief Justice or the judge is asked by the Home Office what period should be served as retribution.

LL: How does your Christianity affect you in this connection?

SP: I do not think that one's religious belief makes any difference in these matters. Christianity does not make any difference. Those judges who I know are agnostics – there are not many – are all in the Christian tradition and have a Christian ethical background and, even if they are agnostic, they cannot escape the atmosphere in which they are brought up in this country.

LL: Are you satisfied on the whole with the way things are handled by the judiciary, or could they be improved?

SP: Parliament lays down the various forms of disposal for those guilty of crimes. Sometimes a new provision is overworked, to the detriment of a more proven system. Suspended prison sentences, for example, as opposed to probation: many courts chose to make suspended sentences which, later, were coupled with a supervision order. The number of people on probation fell dramatically until the Court of Appeal began to lay down guidelines and say 'You can't do this.' Penal reformers are trying to keep people out of prison on account of gross over-crowding, but this should not be the yardstick.

LL: For some reason I have never understood, prison sentences in this country are longer than anywhere else. The present Lord Chief Justice has done his best to reduce sentences and they have been reduced for a number of offences, but at the same time the number of people committing crimes has increased markedly, and we have a lot of very serious criminals around.

SP: I don't know the answer to why judges impose longer sentences. Some crimes offend Christian morals; incest, for example. When I started, a man guilty of incest would expect a minimum of seven years and very likely of ten. With time, the sentence has been reduced, and sometimes they do not go to prison at all, so long as no one is at risk. Things have changed, and perhaps the Christian ethic itself has become more compassionate. It depends on the offence. If you have a man guilty of rape with bodily harm, or one who has a previous history of violence, this is always a difficulty.

LL: If a person has a psychiatric factor and has spent time in a psychiatric hospital, would that carry weight in deciding his sentence?

SP: Of course it would. If it is a mental imbalance coming out, he is very dangerous. If there is medical evidence to that effect, it might well be a case for life imprisonment. If there is live evidence of mental imbalance and I think he is very dangerous, I could not possibly tell when he would be fit to be let loose.

LL: Is there anything else you would like to add?

SP: One of the difficulties in dealing with the mental element in crime is that you start with somebody who has been found guilty. All crimes have some mental element in them, and serious crimes have a serious mental element in them. The finding of guilt by the jury shows that the person was capable of forming the necessary intent. A classic example is that of a drunken man: if the jury thought he was able to pick up a glass and smash it into another man's face, he was able to form an intent, a drunken intent. That is no answer when it comes to passing sentence. If the intent has been influenced by a mental condition, and one of the reasons he formed the intent was because of some mental imbalance, the prime effect on the judge is that he is a dangerous chap, and, for the protection of society, what must be done about it? The mental element is endemic in all crime.

III
Witnesses

I Psychiatrists

Professor Robert Bluglass
Professor of Forensic Psychiatry, University of Birmingham

Professor Bluglass has made such immense contributions to forensic psychiatry in recent years that any quotations from his writings are unlikely to do him justice. Nevertheless, I will quote from two of his articles in the *British Medical Journal*, one entitled 'Recruitment and Training of Prison Doctors' (4 August 1990), and the other 'Mentally Disordered Prisoners: Reports But No Improvements' (25 June 1988).

The first begins by referring to what Professor Bluglass calls 'the disgraceful state of our prisons'. He has no doubt that 'the unsatisfactory working environment inevitably affects recruitment of staff of all kinds and the quality of service', and that the 'Prison Medical Service has long been a cause for concern and the subject of periodic reports'.

He acknowledges that the proposals of a government committee 'should be welcomed; an improvement in the quality and status of prison doctors is long overdue. But without improvements in working conditions, the training of prison nursing staff, and the interlocking of the Prison Medical Service with services for offenders outside prison, how will a career in prison medicine compete with the attractions of alternatives elsewhere?' He concludes that unless conditions for all prisoners are substantially improved 'a few well-trained doctors will continue to struggle to care for their patients in the face of a degree of adversity that will tend to defeat them'.

The second article reminds us that 'since the beginning of the century reports on prisons have conveyed concern for the number of mentally disordered people in prison.' It warns us that 'the proportion of such inmates appears steadily to increase . . . With the decline of the mental hospital and the enthusiastic promotion of community care, more mentally abnormal offenders are likely to find their way into custody.' (His reference to 'enthusiasm' in the promotion of community care must be deemed to be ironical.)

His last paragraph is bleak: 'Little has changed since the *British Medical Journal* produced a series of articles on prisons in 1984; the fundamental causes of all the difficulties remain, and will continue to do so, until the Home Office and the Department of Health and Social Security attack the problem with real determination.'

I asked Professor Bluglass, as I had asked other witnesses, what he would do if he were dictator. His first response was not dissimilar to that of Professor Gunn (see page 48): he would greatly increase the number of regional secure units. He himself is justly proud of his own 100-bed unit in Birmingham. I told him that the average stay in the two regional secure units I had visited was only about six months. He said that some of his residents stayed up to, or longer than, two years. He did not regard it, however, as a long-stay establishment. Such establishments should be provided otherwise. The Professor thought that the prison service should consider providing properly upgraded hospitals of a standard equivalent to the best in the National Health Service for some particular individuals such as those suffering from the legal category of psychopathic disorder, but those who are mentally ill or mentally handicapped should properly be in Health Service provision outside. An increase in the number of regional secure units will have a beneficial effect on reducing the number of mentally disordered who are inappropriately in prisons.

Professor Bluglass attached equal priority, perhaps more, to a complete reform of the Prison Medical Service (PMS). In principle he is in favour of the incorporation of the PMS into the NHS. In the meantime, the recent proposals of a government committee are a big step in the right direction. He entirely agrees with Judge Tumim's (see page 123) recent insistence that the level of psychiatric care in prison hospitals should be brought up to that of hospitals. I pointed out what of course he was already aware of, that the training of the nurses in the latter is vastly superior to that of the prison officers who take on nursing duties in prison hospitals. If he had his way, all of the latter would be trained up to a full nursing standard, as is already the case in the women's prisons. He would like to see a separation of the custodial and the medical functions in prison hospitals.

Professor Bluglass agreed that so far community care had fallen well below the standard expected when the policy of closing the mental hospitals was embarked on, and that the closures should not continue unless accompanied by the equivalent provision in smaller units. The special hospitals should be phased out, and be replaced by smaller units closer to the families of the inmates.

On the theoretical side, I was much interested by his amplification of an article in the *Journal of Forensic Psychiatry* on the role of the psychiatrist as an expert witness in the courts. At present, he explained, a psychiatrist is accepted as an expert witness on 'abnormal', not 'normal', defendants. Even in the case of 'abnormal' patients, however, the function of the forensic psychiatrist is far from clear to me. The forensic psychiatrist is expected to pronounce an opinion on whether 'abnormality' exists. How far he is expected by the courts or by his professional rules to offer an opinion on whether the 'abnormality' caused the crime seems to be a grey area. I believe Professor Bluglass does not consider it unreasonable to expect the forensic psychiatrist to give an opinion on the latter issue.

Professor Bluglass asked me whether I had any message in mind. I said that as I proceeded I became more and more convinced that nothing satisfactory would be accomplished unless the Home Office and the Department of Health were far more co-ordinated in this respect than at present. For this and other reasons it was essential to set up a high-level government inquiry into the whole neglected subject of mental offenders (he does not like that phrase) without further delay. He told me, smilingly, that it seemed to have escaped my notice that such an inquiry had been announced (the Review of Services for Mentally Abnormal Offenders, chaired by Dr John Reed), and that he and Professor Gunn would both be serving on the committee. Its interim report was published near the end of 1991 (see *Postscript*).

Dr Paul Bowden
Forensic Psychiatrist, The Maudsley Hospital

Besides being forensic psychiatrist of the Maudsley Hospital, where he runs an open unit for the treatment of mentally disordered offenders, Dr Paul Bowden has also worked for the last 15 years in Brixton Prison.

Dr Bowden is concerned in particular with those who have killed, looking after them in the period before trial, assisting both the defence and the Crown Prosecution Services, and appearing in court as an expert witness in murder trials. He sees about 80 to 100 defendants a year, and since the mid-1970s, well over 1,000 on murder charges. In addition he acts as adviser to the doctors in Brixton in difficult cases where, for example, people present problems in their management or in cases of hunger strike.

Dr Bowden has tried over the years to draw attention to a number of medical organizations, but his efforts have been thwarted by the Home Office, the Board of Prison Visitors, and various committees. He has learned to be more guarded in his general approach. As the result of an article he wrote in the *Journal of Medical Ethics* on the position of doctors working in prisons – raising the question of how far they should champion the rights of prisoners – he suffered a setback in his work.

More recently, following the spate of suicides in prisons and the revelations about the appalling conditions in Brixton's F-Wing, he gave evidence to the Report of Judge Tumim, Chief Inspector of Prisons, on suicides in prison and to the Council of Europe, who made a tour of inspection there.

In reply to my question about the role of the forensic psychiatrist, and in particular how far it is his or her duty to offer an opinion with regard to the guilt or otherwise of the defendant, Dr Bowden gave an emphatic reply: 'It is never a consideration. English law is quite clear on that point.' The forensic psychiatrist gives his opinion, but juries do not always accept medical evidence; they often have a broader concept of abnormality of mind than an expert. For example, pre-menstrual tension has been accepted as an abnormality of mind, but not drug addiction. It is quite clear in law that the issue of abnormality of mind is for the jury alone. The forensic psychiatrist advises, but the advice is not always accepted. Mental responsibility is not a medical, and even less a psychiatric, issue; it is a legal and a moral one. Legally it refers to liability to punishment, and morally to blameworthiness.

I asked Dr Bowden whether the general body of forensic psychiatrists agreed with his views. He believes that it is naïve to think that all mentally disordered people will ever be kept out of prison. This should be accepted, and proper provision accordingly made for their care. He had arrived at this conclusion after working in prisons for a number of years. There are indeed very few mentally disordered people in prison – hundreds rather than thousands – who should be under the care of the NHS. Dr Bowden has done research in this area and has argued the point in print. There are large numbers of chronic schizophrenics and alcohol abusers, for example, who do not wish to be treated in psychiatric clinics. They either find themselves in prison, or become a nuisance in the community.

In the past, the large mental institutions were in effect prisons. At Horton Hospital in 1930, for example, there were eight abscondencies, while in 1962, after the bars were taken down, the number rose to 207. Dr Bowden stressed that it was not the decline or closure of the mental hospitals which had given rise to current problems, but the opening of them in the first place. There is a distinct need to provide proper resources in prisons. The Home Office insists this is the responsibility of the NHS, which in turn claims that it should be a Home Office responsibility.

Dr Bowden is trying to get an intensive care unit set up in Brixton Prison for acute cases of psychiatric disorder, but is meeting with resistance from the Home Office and the PMS on the grounds that it is an NHS responsibility. Failure to adopt this step results in such prisoners being treated in a most degrading, inhumane way. The hospital in Brixton Prison is largely used for the well-behaved, and sometimes important people with connections. F-Wing is set aside for the unfortunate, the mentally ill, and ethnic minorities. On the ground floor are the 'strip' cells, airless, indescribably filthy and empty of all furniture apart from a mattress. The light is left burning 24 hours a day. These conditions present an extreme form of deprivation, underlying his attempts to set up an intensive care unit.

Dr Bowden said that he had been deeply impressed by the remarks of a member of the Council of Europe group visiting Brixton Prison: 'Help me to understand,' she had pleaded. 'In Europe we look upon England as a liberal country, a model to emulate. I cannot believe what I am seeing here. How can you ill-treat people like this?'

I then returned to the point made earlier by Dr Bowden with regard to the limited function of the forensic psychiatrist. He explained that it is rare for a link to be drawn between mental disorder and the criminal act. When he states in court that the defendant is a schizophrenic for whom he can find a place in a secure unit which will accept him, nobody raises the issue of the link between schizophrenia and the crime. He himself does not express any opinion as to what is best for the man. 'Mad or bad' are not comparable values.

Dr Bowden said that the fact that someone is mentally ill does not mean they are absolved from responsibility. It would depend on an intimate understanding of the nature of their illness and the behaviour that led to the criminal act. Many mentally ill people commit criminal offences for reasons unconnected with their mental state. There are differing relationships between the mental disorder and the crime: in some cases there is no relationship; in others the connection is complete, but there is an infinite variety of links between them.

Take for example the case of a man plagued by auditory hallucinations which he resists, struggles against for years, consults doctors, but is finally overwhelmed by and kills. Then, on the other hand, that of a man who, in response to his first hallucination, succumbs and kills without any resistance. Are they equally responsible? Dr Bowden believes one must understand intimately the nature of the mental disorder and the way in which it affects the thinking and behaviour of each case, and link it with the crime. This is rarely done.

I was of the opinion that in court, where people are being sentenced, a moral judgment has to be made by someone. Dr Bowden explained that the problem created by an intensive inquiry into the state of mind of the criminal linked with the crime is that it conflicts with our adversarial criminal justice system, which sees everything in black and white.

Dr Bowden sees psychiatry as deterministic: the more that is known about people's lives, the better we are able to understand them. He has seen most of the major killers over the last 15 years, and all of the men who have killed their children. He cited the case of a man who killed his daughter in a most horrible way. He had been brought up confined in a shed, beaten, and deprived in every way. He had grown up devoid of all feelings, which had enabled him to survive. At his trial he was treated as a pariah. Dr Bowden endeavoured to introduce some ideas into his evidence to help the court to understand. The judge stopped him: it was essential that the defendant be made to appear as an animal. Was he as responsible as you or I? That is why determinism – bringing in life experience and heredity, trying to explain human behaviour – assists the course of human justice.

I questioned whether it was necessary to change people who commit terrible deeds. Dr Bowden replied that if the courts were to allow that not everyone accepts free will, they would find life too difficult and would not be able to take it on board.

Dr Bowden was then asked, if he were a dictator, what would he do? What would his priorities be? His reply was unequivocal: 'If I were a dictator, I would abolish dictatorships! I would provide psychiatric treatment units within prisons, which are non-existent now. They would be designated as hospitals under the Health Service Acts and consist of small intensive care units. When people were ill in prison we would treat them properly, instead of as now treating them like animals.'

I wondered whether a debate on the matter in the House of Lords might be productive, but Dr Bowden did not think that if the NHS took things over, they would be any better. To call doctors in from outside would not necessarily be the right solution. Staff in these units would not always be fully trained nurses. A mix of skills would be good. Dr Bowden envisaged numbers in these units as being no more than seven or eight at a time. Places in these special units would be of a temporary nature – say, for a month.

Dr Bowden gave the example of a man who had been brought into prison recently and had remained mute since his arrest. He had killed and dismembered his common-law wife. He had not spoken one word since his arrest beyond occasionally chanting, 'Why? Why?

Why?' He was sent to Manchester where he spent some time in hospital, psychotic and catatonic. He now lies naked on a mattress in an empty cell, the light always burning. No other resources or facilities exist for dealing with him. Dr Bowden is trying to get him transferred to a special hospital, but nobody will come to see him first. The man will have to remain there at least for another week before this is done. Everything depends on the hospital agreeing to accept him. Dr Bowden is unable to treat him for two reasons: he wishes the man to be ill when he is assessed, and he cannot sedate him because he is not properly monitored.

Dr Bowden wants a unit so that these people can be properly treated and no longer locked up in this sort of environment: 'We need an input into the prisons, now!'

Dr Henrietta Bullard
Forensic Psychiatrist, Fairmile Hospital

Dr Henrietta Bullard is the widow of Dr Hamilton, who was Superintendent of Broadmoor. She is a highly qualified forensic psychiatrist, one of a select band of whom, when I saw her, there were only about 60 in Great Britain.

The regional secure unit at the Fairmile Hospital, Wallingford, contains 15 beds, 13 of them occupied at the time of my visit. The atmosphere was pleasantly relaxed. I retain a vivid memory of a charming young woman who, I was told, was an occupational therapist. I assumed she was a member of the staff, but it turned out she was a patient. I learned later that she had killed two of her children and tried to kill herself.

The question of who goes and who should go to a regional secure unit is not an easy one to answer. In a debate on mentally ill offenders which I initiated in the House of Lords in 1984, the Minister, Lord Elton, spoke in this way: 'Our view is that decisions on admissions are for those running the units to take, having regard to the particular behavioural problems of individuals, the majority of whom are likely to be suffering from some form or other of mental disorder, and their likely response to treatment.'

Lord Allen of Abbeydale pursued the matter further in an intervention. 'There is a well-understood policy as to who goes to Broadmoor, Rampton and the other two special hospitals. One would hope that there might be a similar policy for the regional units; evidently there is not.' Lord Elton replied: 'I think that this is something which may develop in time, but at the moment every case is carefully discussed. It may be that, with experience, those in the newer regional secure units will come to recognize the cases and some transfers will be made as a matter of course, but that is an aspiration and not a prediction.'

Dr Bullard holds a strong belief that some longer-term units should be established and hopes herself to establish a unit with 100 beds at Oxford, in place of the three present regional secure units with 49 designated secure beds. I noticed that Lord Elton, in the debate quoted from, told the House that, 'It is expected that patients will

remain in their unit for not longer than eighteen months to two years.'
Both at Hellingly Regional Secure Unit in East Sussex and at
Fairmile the average stay seems to be of the order of six months. I
myself make the assumption that regional secure units are a fine
development. I accept the demand of Professor Gunn (page 48), for
example, that the beds should be increased from the present 600 to
the 2,000 (for offender-patients) recommended by the Butler Committee. The difficulties, however, of achieving any such target are
highlighted by Dr Bullard's own experience. I will quote from a letter
to me:

> Although we have to run the service, we have no budget and no
> say as to how the money is spent. I have never seen a budget
> statement and am very aware that money earmarked for the
> Forensic Society Service is being used for other projects within the
> Mental Illness Unit . . . I have also made recommendations about
> the need for long-stay intensive care for patients who require some
> level of security. The patients are usually unlikely to become
> suitable for discharge into the community.

Dr Bullard has not hesitated to point out the difficulties under which
she is now labouring. It is impossible, for example, to recruit a
consultant forensic psychiatrist at Milton Keynes, one of the three
Oxford units. There is also an unfortunate reluctance by the regional
health authority to make any plans for the future of the secure unit
programme, when Fairmile Hospital and Borocourt Hospital close.
As other large hospitals close within the region, there is certain to be
a crisis in the provision of appropriate facilities for offender patients.
Inevitably these people will be diverted to the prison system. Why has
there been so much dragging of feet towards the creation of regional
secure units? If it is due to local unpopularity, that is not a satisfactory
excuse.

Henrietta Bullard complains, incidentally, about the difficulty of
recruiting adequate staff, but does not hesitate to inform us, for
example, that the ratio at Fairmile is 36 nurses to 13 patients, and
other staff are additional. The ratio is obviously much higher than
that which prevails in hospitals or prisons. One has to be very
sure, as I am, of the particular service that can be rendered by

regional secure units to demand the staff required by them.

Let it not be forgotten that the staff in regional secure units are trained nurses. It is no disparagement of nursing officers in prisons or, for that matter, of prison staff without nursing training, to suggest that the services rendered by the nurses in the regional secure units, given the high ratio of staff to patients, are not likely to be equalled elsewhere. Let us therefore accept that they are centres of excellence, and press on with the demand that the original conception of the Butler Committee be realized.

Professor John Gunn

Professor of Forensic Psychiatry, Institute of Psychiatry

Professor Gunn is the only professor of forensic psychiatry in Britain funded by the Universities' Funding Council. He is sharply critical of the educational provision for forensic psychiatry:

> My criticism is less of the Department of Education and Science and more of the system by which educational monies are allocated to universities. The biggest problem at the moment is of course a very serious shortage of university funds, which removes all flexibility at the local level. However, there has never been a way in which another government department, say, the Home Office, or the Department of Health, can approach the Department of Education and Science for differential funding in any needy area. Hence there is no way of remedying the current problem of academic forensic psychiatry.

The fact that he and Professor Bluglass are the only professors of forensic psychiatry is indicative of attitudes to research in this subject. The Department of Health is usually castigated in this connection, and Professor Gunn wished me to realize that the Ministry of Education is, in its own way, just as culpable.

A document produced by the directors of MIND, the National Schizophrenia Fellowship, the Howard League, the Prison Reform Trust and the National Association for the Care and Resettlement of Offenders (NACRO) was sent to the Home Secretary on 10 July 1990. Professor Gunn was quoted in a manner that he found unsatisfactory. They said that in 1972, in a previous survey, he had estimated that one-third of prisoners would benefit from psychiatric care. The document implied that these prisoners were mentally vulnerable (not a term he used himself), and should be transferred from prison to hospital. In fact, he had estimated that between 1 and 2 percent of the prison population should be transferred from prison to hospital on mental grounds. Even so, that could amount to up to 700 patients requiring specialist treatment within the NHS.

The fact that the number requiring transfer was far less than that suggested in the joint letter did not make the need for their transfer any less urgent. Professor Gunn agreed with those who asserted that a number of persons were in prison today who some years ago would have been in hospital. I felt he was somewhat less ready than Dr Tidmarsh (see page 54) to acquit the psychiatrists in the hospitals for their reluctance to accept mental offenders. He explained their attitude, however, by laying the main blame on successive governments that had starved the health service of funds. Among patients, mental offenders were inevitably at the bottom of the heap, or last in the queue. I suggested that a Labour Government might be more generous towards the health service; he gave me a somewhat sceptical look, but accepted the possibility:

> I am not certain that the problems of transfer would be solved simply by the addition of more beds. Another important factor is attitudes. Currently NHS doctors are extremely reluctant to treat mentally abnormal offenders, especially those they label as 'personality disordered'. Overcoming this particular problem requires much more extensive educational programmes, and we are back at the problem of university funding.

In regard to the health service generally, Professor Gunn stressed two points: the ageing of the population; and technological development and the ever-increasing expenditure involved. 'I suspect,' he said, 'that governments do understand the two points I make about health inflation. What they fail to do, however, is to fund at that level. Increments to the health service tend to be based much more on the overall inflation percentage, and this leaves health with an increasing deficit.'

I told Professor Gunn that Dr Tidmarsh had called for a halt to the running-down of the mental hospitals. In this he would appear to be supported by penal reformers generally. Professor Gunn thought the matter was not quite so simple:

> I am not one of those who supports the notion of keeping large outdated mental hospitals open. They had many deficiencies from the beginning, and now are not places which provide appropriate management for many of our patients. What I am very critical of

is that the funds locked up in those mental hospitals are not transferred into new psychiatric services, which would enable the patients to have a better quality of care. In my experience in the south, most districts are now very short of funds for psychiatric care, and have not benefited from the closure of mental hospitals in their own district.

I was much interested, and perhaps a little surprised, to learn of Professor Gunn's enthusiasm for the regional secure units, and, incidentally, for the Butler Report of 1975. He pointed out that the Report had called for 2,000 places in the regional secure units. We now have only 600, despite endless assertions by governments of their belief in such units. I asked him if the whole picture would be transformed if we could achieve the original target of 2,000 places: 'I am not sure that I would agree with the word "transformed" for the full implementation of the Butler proposals. Certainly things would be markedly improved, but for a full transformation I think we should have to add many other new services and improve the educational ones as well.'

Professor Gunn did not feel that the Mental Health Act of 1983 needed alteration. The legal cover was there if proper use were made of the Act. But, as explained above, the responsibility for not using it, while directly attached to the psychiatrists in the hospitals, must ultimately be placed on the shoulders of the governments that failed to provide the necessary resources.

We discussed the concept of psychopathy, which he told me was not a medical term. He feels it is possible to provide medical assistance to persons of disordered personality. I asked him whether Hitler was mad or bad. He felt the concept was of value, and later wrote:

We did not discuss my views on 'mad or bad' very much, so you might like a brief expansion. I don't think that the either/or dichotomy is appropriate. We all use moral language and concepts in our everyday life. It is almost inconceivable to imagine human discourse without morality. We will therefore attach moral value to everything human, and in the moral dimension, Hitler and his like clearly have to be at the very bad end of the spectrum.

Psychiatrists, on the other hand, have technical language which is disconnected from moral language and is morally neutral. Mental illness does not in itself have a moral value, nor does it in my view excuse in a moral sense. In court, psychiatrists are necessarily embroiled in all kinds of curious discussions about 'responsibility', legal excuses, and the like, but in their own world they make a distinction between morality and illness, such that it is possible to describe an act as part of an illness and good, or part of an illness and bad, or healthy and good, or healthy and bad. So it is perfectly possible to describe acts, and people, from different perspectives. The health perspective and the moral perspective are simply different ways of construing the universe, and it is perfectly possible to switch the language from one to another.

While I follow the Professor's distinction, I am puzzled as to how it could be used as a basis for sentencing by a court. Professor Gunn says that mental illness does not excuse in a moral sense. I should have thought that most people, including most judges, regard it as diminishing the guilt of the defendant, and therefore calling for specialized treatment. This in practice surely produces a better life for defendants found to be mentally ill than their fellows get – for example, Ronnie Kray is better treated in Broadmoor than is Reggie, his brother, in prison. Ian Brady too is better treated in Ashworth than he was in prison. Is Professor Gunn saying that psychiatrists should be concerned entirely with what treatment is best for the patient? Would he agree this is the recognized viewpoint of his profession?

I asked him, as I have others, what he would do if he was medical dictator. He gave an authoritative, if rather overpowering reply:

I would increase resources to forensic psychiatry very significantly. . . . I would give special priority to university funding, but I would also double or treble the current level of basic forensic psychiatry funding at the district level. This means I would try to approach the recommendations made by the Butler Committee in 1974.

Further, I would ensure that proper rehabilitation services were available for our patients to move on to. This would mean an adequate provision of supervised hostels, sheltered workshops, day hospitals, and long-stay beds in general psychiatric units. None of these is adequately supplied at present. I would further add medium-security beds which were not only for short-term use, as at present. I would like to see the development of brand new services within the health sector, such as special facilities for sexually deviant patients, and therapeutic community facilities a bit like Grendon Prison.

A special urgent need at the moment is for services for drug addicts and alcoholics. These need not necessarily be run by doctors, but they would have to have some links with the health system. In this list, I don't think I am calling for anything particularly contentious. I think, however, the length of the list and the despair one has in spelling it out, shows the enormous gap there is between current provision and ideal provision.

When my book was further advanced I approached Professor Gunn again and he took the trouble to amplify what he had told me earlier:

I am pressing hard for the Home Office to publish our report on sentenced mentally disordered prisoners as soon as possible. In the meantime, let me explain that we tried to estimate the unmet psychiatric needs of sentenced prisoners in England and Wales and estimated that a considerable number of prisoners currently serving sentences should in fact be transferred to NHS psychiatric hospitals. As we were only able to interview a sample of prisoners we have to estimate this number from the proportion we found in our sample, and the estimation falls between 756 and 1,371. Lots of people are now interpreting this as saying we have found 'around 1,000' prisoners who require hospital attention. These prisoners will require all levels of security within the NHS, but it did seem we could safely say that approximately one-third of them would need maximum security, a further third medium security, and the final third could be managed in ordinary psychiatric care.

I asked Professor Gunn about 'all types of psychiatric attention required by prisoners'. He replied:

A gross simplification/condensation of our results is that approximately 25 percent of all sentenced prisoners require some form of psychiatric assistance; about 11 percent could get that from visiting doctors to the prison providing 'out-patient' treatment; another 6 percent would require treatment in therapeutic communities of one kind or another, like Grendon Prison; 3 percent should be moved out of the prisons into the health service; and a further 5 percent we were unable to specify because we believe that the patients would require further assessment for proper treatment decisions to be made.

Professor Gunn confirmed my assumption that the various figures were referring to *convicted* prisoners: 'That is all we studied. That is all we were asked to study. We are currently beginning negotiations with the Home Office to see whether a similar study of remanded prisoners would be useful and feasible.' Professor Gunn's report on sentenced mentally disordered prisoners was published near the end of 1991 (see *Postscript*).

Dr Ian Keitch
Director of Medical Services, Rampton Hospital

I began by asking Dr Keitch about the composition of the population at Rampton. It is no longer a hospital mainly devoted to sub-normal mental patients; about two-thirds are not sub-normal and one-third is. Of the entire British population in special hospitals, one-half of the sub-normal patients are in Rampton, and one-quarter of the others. The population of Rampton has decreased in the last ten years from 1,100 to 550.

I asked Dr Keitch about the Mental Health Act of 1983. He saw no need to change it, although it was subject to many varied interpretations. Dr Keitch said that while there was no difficulty in diagnosing the mentally ill, the difficulty began with the psychopath. He and five of his staff would sit round the table to decide whether a particular candidate was suitable for Rampton under the terms of the Act. If they adopted a very liberal interpretation, Rampton would be filled to overflowing in three weeks. At the moment they are adopting a middle-of-the-road interpretation, and no doubt they would be more liberal if more facilities were available.

This led me to ask Dr Keitch what he would do if he were a dictator in this field. He began by distinguishing four kinds of provision for mental offenders: first, maximum security, for example Rampton, Broadmoor, etc.; second, medium security in the form of regional secure units; third, minimal security in mental hospitals, apart from regional secure units; fourth, no security, but care in the community. I told him that Professor Gunn (see page 48) had placed his prime emphasis on increasing the regional secure units up to the Butler Committee level. Dr Keitch agreed with this, but his own emphasis was on expansion of the provision in the ordinary mental hospitals. He was not in favour of increasing the provision in special hospitals.

When I told him that Dr David Tidmarsh (see page 55) and many penal reformers blame the running down of the mental hospitals for the increased number of prisoners, Dr Keitch thought there was something in this, though too much should not be read into it. He agreed that some of the mental hospitals were too large and antiquated, and smaller units would be more helpful.

Dr Keitch was very anxious to see much improved provision in the community. If he were a dictator, he said he would introduce community treatment orders, which would enable the authorities to control patients while they were still in the community. Finally, if he were allowed only one sentence in which to express his aspirations it would be this: 'To provide asylum for all those in need of it.' He was using the word 'asylum' in very broad terms, almost equivalent, I think, to what others would call care. Dr Keitch has a deep conviction that there are a number of people who would always need full protection, and it might well be in some kind of hospital.

After our meeting, Dr Keitch supplied me with a document called *Prejudice and Pride*, the report of an official inquiry into Rampton Hospital in October 1989, which is a review of the outcome of the Boynton Report of October 1980. In it, the inquiry team refer to their awareness of 'the almost universal prejudice about Rampton Hospital, which usually comes from ignorance'. Yet they also found among the people working in the hospital a fierce pride in what they were doing, and an aim to work to the highest professional standards. They passed a very favourable verdict on the work done by the hospital in the last decade.

A closely argued discussion at the end of the report asks whether Rampton Hospital should close. In favour of keeping it open, the team conclude there is no reason to close it: 'It is still meeting an essential need in the national system for the management of mentally abnormal offenders, and there is no obvious practical model which could replace it.' However, they do not seem very happy with their own conclusion: 'It is a very long time since this model of care was devised, and it is time to think deeply on what is to take its place.'

The team describe various models and decide in favour of what they call the 'territorial' model, which integrates local and special services. It includes the occasional need for special security, intermediate security in regional secure units, contacts with prison medical services, magistrates' courts, probation officers, alcohol and drug misuse services, and with all kinds of statutory and voluntary agencies. In this model, the special hospital becomes a provider of an essential part of a comprehensive service which can be purchased by the health authority.

Dr David Tidmarsh

Consultant Psychiatrist, Broadmoor Hospital; Senior Lecturer, Institute of Psychiatry

I began by recalling our debate in the House of Lords in November 1988 in which I had expressed the view that many people were in prison who should be in hospital, or looked after in the community. Professor Gunn, who I was seeing the following day, for the last five years had been conducting a major inquiry into these issues. Dr Tidmarsh assisted Professor Gunn (see page 46) in the inquiry, and regarded the conclusions of Gunn as providing the best answers – that there are a number (probably hundreds rather than thousands) of mentally disordered prisoners who should be transferred to hospital or back into the community – although problems of definition would remain.

Dr Tidmarsh does not consider diagnosis as proving difficult in the case of the most common mental illnesses. He admitted, however, that there could be real difficulty in deciding whether someone was psychopathic or suffered from other forms of mental disorder. I suggested that the types often cited as examples of psychopathy were similar to those that the general public associated with people like Hitler or Saddam Hussein.

Dr Tidmarsh stressed the problems presented by drug addiction and alcoholism. Drug addicts suffer from an overwhelming need to obtain drugs, and for most people this can only be achieved by stealing. He felt much more work had to be done on and with such people.

As a very caring doctor, Dr Tidmarsh looks at the treatment of individuals from the point of view of their needs – although he is not, of course, unaware of the legal and social issues involved – which seem to mean that mental offenders should be transferred to hospital when there is some hope of treatment proving effective.

Dr Tidmarsh said he had a number of sex offenders in Broadmoor as patients and that he would be ready to transfer such people from prison if and when more effective treatment becomes available. He agreed that a number of mental offenders were now in prison who some years ago would have been in hospital. He did not, however, accept the argument that psychiatrists are now less confident of treating, for instance, psychopaths; he laid the responsibility on successive governments that have been, and still are, engaged in running down the mental hospitals.

When asked what he would do if he were a dictator in this field, he had no doubt at all: overwhelming priority should be given to stopping the process of running down. He thought that two influences had been at work in producing this disastrous development. On the one hand, the permissiveness of the 1960s, that is, the idea of giving people freedom at all costs; on the other hand, the Thatcherite emphasis of the last ten years on reducing expenditure.

Dr Tidmarsh mentioned that larger units are on the whole more economical than smaller ones. Alternatively, adequate community care, of which there is no sign at the moment, would in his view be of no financial benefit, which does not mean he is not in favour of much more generous provision of this kind.

The overwhelming need is to provide more facilities in the psychiatric hospitals and better community care. Dr Tidmarsh does not favour an increase in the number of special hospitals. If he had his way, a number of prisoners would be transferred to such hospitals, but a number of special hospital patients would be transferred to ordinary mental hospitals, or into community care.

Professor John Wing
Director of Research Unit, Royal College of Psychiatrists

Professor Wing has contributed greatly to the treatment of mental patients and ex-mental patients. He would not, I think, claim to have specialized in mental offenders, but he would, I think, agree with Professor Gunn (see page 46) that more adequate treatment of mental offenders depends on more adequate provision for mental patients and ex-mental patients generally.

Professor Wing has written and spoken much on these matters, notably in his essay 'Vision and Reality' in the book *The Closure of Powick Hospital*. The views he expressed to me in the interview are set out systematically in that essay; I will summarize them briefly below.

Professor Wing selects 1954 as a crucial date:

> The peak of bed occupancy (after a more or less steady rise throughout the country) occurred in 1954. 'Rundown' began earlier in the pioneering hospitals, but it first became visible in the national statistics in 1955. It has continued ever since. This was not a top-down policy decision but was due to the introduction of social methods of rehabilitation and resettlement by pioneering doctors, nurses and social workers, followed by the first really effective medications.

The last phrase refers to the remarkable progress made about that time in the development of drugs for dealing with mental patients. Professor Wing goes on to say that closure plans began to be formulated in the late 1950s. He agreed with me that the new permissive philosophy that dominated the 1960s played its part in addition to the factors mentioned. Professor Wing looks back on the subsequent thirty years with guarded approval. The crucial question he asks is, how far has the vision been fulfilled?

The following passage must be quoted in full, because without it one cannot adequately understand the richness of Professor Wing's conception. He refers to three principles which contribute to his vision of best practice in community psychiatry:

First, it should be based on state-of-the-art knowledge of the causes of social disablement associated with the manifestations of mental illness or handicap. Second, on knowledge of the ways in which such causative or sustaining factors can be prevented, reduced or contained. Third, on an understanding of how staff and services can most effectively identify people with mental health problems, assess their needs for various forms of treatment, enabling and care, and meet these through the provision of services that do not themselves impose further disability.

The third of these principles itself has three parts. A community service should be geographically responsible, so that it can be based on an epidemiological understanding of local needs. It should be comprehensive, with a range of facilities and skilled staff, wide enough and flexible enough to cope with the variety of need. It should be integrated with an organization and administration capable of ensuring adequate continuity of care with economy and efficiency.

The concept of ladders or stairways is useful in formulating both the functions and the possible structures of services. Residential, occupational and recreational needs can be visualized in terms of three stairways, each with landings at different functional levels, with rooms leading off for recuperation and rehabilitation. At the bottom of all three are facilities for severely disabled people with the highest dependency needs. Those who reach the top have no need of any specialist services. The stairways have aids to help disabled people to mount at an appropriate pace or (if all the steps are in place) to prevent a precipitate fall to the bottom at times of relapse. These aids – assessment, treatment, enabling, care, welfare supplements, special support – are provided by professional and informal carers.

These are tremendous aspirations. Professor Wing is by no means pessimistic in regard to their realization since that time. 'Seen from a thirty-year perspective, one must conclude that progress towards community care defined in terms of services that are both independent of large hospitals and better than the best available when the ideas were being formulated, has been promising but not spectacular.' He is aware of the widespread criticism of the extent of the community care provided in the meanwhile. He told me that psychiatrists had had a rough passage in recent years, though he thought the climate was now improving.

When I asked Professor Wing what he would do if he were medical dictator today, he laid enormous stress on the ear-marking by the central government of the funds made available for mental illness to the regional health authorities or the local authorities. There lies a simple political issue. More fundamentally, his whole conception of community care has got to be understood if one is going to do justice to his thinking. It is fatal, in his view, to talk of emptying the mental hospitals and leaving the former patients to be looked after in the community. In other words, a sharp line must not be drawn between hospital and community care.

He rejected a simple policy of closing the mental hospitals, but that did not mean that he would keep them all going. Some of them should be used as the centres of the new community service. It would have been far easier and more profitable to do this years ago, but it is still not too late.

On the administrative side, Professor Wing would like to see mental after-care under unified control. He would prefer it to be in the hands of the health authorities. The government have opted for the local authorities. No doubt Professor Wing would insist on maximum co-ordination, knowing full well the difficulties involved.

II Representatives

Ian Bynoe
Legal Director, The National Association for Mental Health (MIND)

MIND works to promote the interests and views of people diagnosed as mentally ill. Mental offenders are, of course, only one part of their concern, but, to quote Ian Bynoe, 'MIND's legal department, through its links with lawyers and the Forensic Psychiatric Service, possesses a close and individual interest in the developments in the criminal justice and penal system, and in the prison medical service.'

MIND has established itself as the leading organization in Britain which deals with mental illness: it has brought much public pressure to bear on behalf of the mentally ill; it gave very important evidence to the inquiry of the chief inspector of prisons into prison suicides; and it has provided invaluable briefing to members of the House of Commons and the House of Lords.

Broadly speaking, the submission of MIND falls under four headings:

- The need to transfer a considerable number of mentally disordered offenders from prison to hospital.
- The need to bring about transfers much more rapidly than at present.
- The need for a vast improvement in the medical service provided in prisons for the mentally ill.
- The need for a far-reaching development of the provision in hospitals and in the community for the mentally ill.

Mr Bynoe himself considers that the diversion from custody of the mentally disturbed or vulnerable offenders 'brings under review three "groups"'. The first consists of those who should not have been prosecuted or should not have entered the criminal justice system at all. The second consists of those who should be prosecuted, but whose mental health needs, both before and after sentence, render a remand

into custody or sentence of imprisonment inappropriate and unjust.
Mr Bynoe adds that 'If the Prison Medical Service provided a service
as good as the National Health Service, then the argument for
transfer or diversion would immediately evaporate.' The third
consists of those who remain in the prison system: 'Clearly much can
be done for this group by a significant improvement of environmental
standards and staffing in prisons, particularly in the squalid local jails.
There is a need for a special care unit as well . . .'

I began by asking Mr Bynoe what was thought to be the scale of the
problem when talking about transferring prisoners to hospital. 'John
Gunn's figure of 1,000 may include people having a neurotic mental
illness. Traditionally the Mental Health Act is not used to treat
neurotic mental illness . . . You may get such patients in hospital a
long time. I imagine Gunn's figure is about right. The number of
those who would certainly benefit from hospital care might not be
the same as the Mental Health Act says should be transferred.
Consent is the issue which is forgotten in much of this. Psychiatric
treatment is ideally now provided on the basis of consent, and doctors
are reluctant to base themselves on a strategy involving compulsion.
This can lead to difficulties for the patient with special needs.' In
general, psychiatrists are keen not to use compulsion as part of the
treatment régime. Psychiatrists are not quoting the Mental Health
Act all the time, but patients are not admitted to regional secure units
unless under the Mental Health Act.

In what follows, Mr Bynoe and I are talking of those who have been
convicted, leaving out of account those on remand.

Lord
Longford:

In the House of Lords recently the matter of the
document signed by the five directors of Penal Reform
Associations was raised. The impression was left that
thousands of prisoners should be transferred.

Ian Bynoe:

I can't give a figure. It probably is around the Gunn
figure [1,000], but I don't believe all those will be
transferable under the Mental Health Act. Those
transferred from prison into the health service would
take their problems with them – drug and alcohol

addiction, personality difficulties, family relationships, and so on. The health service does not want to be involved with that sort of thing.

LL: If you were dictator, what would you do? Professor Gunn would increase the number of regional secure units from 600 to the Butler recommendation of 2,000.

IB: So would I. Double them, treble them. I would like to make them more integrated, more flexible. Many would have patients up to two years, rather than what we normally talk about, that is, one year.

The right policy is one involving fluid security, fashioned to the individual needs of the client. The two things would dictate where they would be placed in the system. At regional secure units like Wrayside they have tried to reduce the prominence of security, while at Broadmoor they have more security than they did ten years ago. There is a large number of patients who do not need maximum security but who are being held on a level of security out of proportion to their needs. It should be variable. At least 800 of the 1,700 people in special hospitals do not need maximum security at that level. As far as their therapeutic needs are concerned, they have no reason to stay any longer.

LL: The argument I come across repeatedly is that they would like to move them out of mental hospitals, but there is no room for them elsewhere and so they have to stay in the special hospitals.

IB: Either the special hospitals take a patient from maximum security to release into the community, or they limit their role to maximum security and give others the job of rehabilitation. Other countries manage their patients requiring maximum security by having smaller units. I recently visited some acute words in a heavily drug-orientated unit. The person with problems in a number of dimensions, not simply mental illness, will not be helped by a drug-orientated régime and little else. The multidisciplinary approach of matching psychiatric social work, specialized nursing, with psychiatry, which is available to clients in regional secure units, can be effective. The important thing is how you deliver an integrated service to the person who has a number of different problems.

The quality of decision-making has a part to play. Courts need to be reined in from making bad decisions, or given powers to obtain information, or require co-operation from others. Some people fail to be where they should because of bad decisions by the courts, which discriminate against a seriously disturbed or vulnerable defendant in a way which would not happen to a person suffering from a physical illness.

Resources are the main agent of change in getting courts to make better decisions. The duty psychiatrist scheme is one of the essential and most valuable means by which a court can improve its decisions. It not only gets information, but the people involved in the scheme have access to services; they are not just experts, they are experts who can fix the making of arrangements alternative to prosecution, remand in custody, imprisonment, getting the health service into the courts. Too often the health service is reluctant even to visit prisons.

LL: The PMS should be integrated with the NHS?

IB: Why does the NHS not provide the service?

LL: You go for flat-out integration?

IB: I don't see arguments against it; I'm against half-hearted schemes.

LL: Do you see any possibility of giving treatment thera-peutically in prison where people are being sent for punishment? Do you see any conflict?

IB: The issue again is consent. Treatment for the person who has psychosexual problems is almost wholly dependent on consent and co-operation. These treatment techniques simply do not require a hospital environment with nursing staff and so on. The main issue is, do you provide the therapeutic treatments in the prison system as at Grendon? Or do you say to the health service: you do it and we will transfer our prisoners into your service? Clearly there is an obvious and demonstrable need for more facilities not met in the prison service, and rarely met satisfactorily in the health service.

People develop distress within the prison system, which has no facilities for giving urgent intensive care, apart from drugs and seclusion. The old way was to warehouse people in large dependency-creating units. The new must strive to meet their individual needs, however intensive. Multidisciplinary teams can approach this task. I am not a great believer in the medical approach.

The future must be right at the 'lino' level – when the patient wishes to complain, his grievances must be properly investigated. An independent body must be responsible for this. There must be no discouragement to making complaints. When a patient needs legal advice and advocacy, will it be available to him? Will the patient's right to privacy and to a personal sexual life be respected?

People in special hospitals are treated unkindly and suffer damage, so there is an incentive not to complain and less opportunity for making complaints than in prison. The chances of treatment being ineffective are increased when the patient is stripped of a sense of dignity and self-worth. The same standard of care should be provided in prison as outside in the community.

Ian Bynoe finds Judge Tumim's proposal (see page 123) for psychiatric units at NHS standard in prisons as an interim measure quite unrealistic. There is a need for emergency intensive care, provided away from prison and the punitive environment. But to raise a unit to NHS standards for a mental hospital under the Act would eliminate all connection with the prison apart from the stone walls.

LL: What is going to be the provision for the 25 percent of prisoners mentioned by our authority as requiring psychiatric treatment?

IB: A medical service provided by the NHS comparable to that available in the community, tailored to prison restrictions. The prison environment causes prisoners to develop anxiety and severe depression. Specialized psychiatric and psychotherapeutic treatments help those with psychosexual problems, and present those wishing to change with the chance to do so.

                  The principle needs to be established that when a court believes that it has to sentence a defendant with a mental disorder, then it must obtain the opinion of a doctor before so doing. That opinion must judge the appropriateness of imprisonment and its effect on treatment. This was actually the import of our recent amendment tabled in the House of Commons which, it seems, the government has finally agreed to.

LL: Where does the special emphasis come in the prisons?

IB: There should be a special unit where prisoners can get psychiatric help. People should not be forced to receive such treatment; it should be voluntary. Judge Tumim speaks of a sort of sick-bay treatment when a prisoner is waiting to leave. There may be a place in the prison system where the Mental Health Act could be used temporarily to provide for a prisoner's need in acute emergency.

                  An important point is that in the prison system a prisoner is entitled to civil rights which enable him to take up issues with the government. In the hospital system complaints must be routed through a doctor.

The hospital régime is infantilizing. There is a great need to ensure that care and treatment are provided without repeating the past mistakes of the big institutions which infantilized their patients.

Harry Fletcher

Assistant General Secretary, The National Association of Probation Officers

Mr Fletcher began by saying that a main piece of work at the moment is concerned with interviewing staff in local and remand prisons, asking their opinions and estimates of the number of prisoners currently in gaol who are in some way mentally disordered.

Mr Fletcher had conducted a pilot scheme on six prisons, and found 2 to 3 percent of the prison population clinically ill and in need of the type of care that is not currently available in the prison system. In one prison, with a population of just under 500, 15 were so ill as to need total care. Mr Fletcher's final figure of the mentally ill, addiction, and personality disorder cases was 20 percent. This is broadly comparable with other findings.

Since the mid-1980s the number of inmates with personality disorders – psychiatric and serious problems of addiction – has erupted. The cases tend to be men and women with fairly short sentences, 18 months or so, arising from damage to property, street fighting, and so on.

Mr Fletcher agreed there was a possible link between the closing down of the mental hospitals and the absence of community care which accounted for this. Prison was aggravating the conditions of these people since they were not receiving any form of treatment. There was a wide range of symptoms: paranoia, refusing food, aggressive behaviour, and odd ideas and behaviour. Prison officers are not trained to deal with mentally ill offenders.

Mr Fletcher then referred to the increasing number of suicides in prison – there had been two more the previous weekend, and the total for 1990 so far was 34. During the previous month there had been five, and he had been able to trace the previous psychiatric history of four of them. All had been receiving treatment, either as in-patients or as out-patients of some institution. Two-thirds of the total had been on remand. His general conclusions were that a considerable number of these afflicted people should be transferred out of prison, while the rest should be given proper care in prison.

Mr Fletcher referred to an article in the *Correspondent* by David

Brindle (13–15 September 1990), which stated that a number of the inmates in special hospitals should not be there at all, but in a range of community facilities – which do not yet exist. About 700 of the prison population are chronically ill, and should be in special hospitals. Brindle estimated that for 1989 the total number of men and women going through the system was about 100,000 (sentenced and remanded). About 15,000 of these were mentally ill in the broadest sense of the term. At least half, or between one-half and two-thirds, had been involved in offences of a non-violent nature, i.e., drug addiction, theft, property offences, criminal damage, drunkenness, and so on. Brindle gave a typical example of one young man, 30 years of age, charged with non-payment of a bill for a meal of £1.40. He was homeless and rootless. Unable to pay the fine, he was sentenced to three months. The implication is that he was mentally disordered.

The need for the provision of alternative community care is becoming more and more apparent. Mr Fletcher said he was getting a lot of case histories of men and women who were mentally ill and should not be in prison. His official line is that as many of the 15,000 as possible should be diverted to community placement. Courts continue to send the bulk to prison because there is no other alternative.

All prisons have the problems of a massive total through-put, in and out. A prison like Wormwood Scrubs, for instance, with a population of 1,400, had 30,000 movements a year. Mentally ill people in need of some kind of assistance are unlikely to receive it because the numbers are so great. Staff are unable to interview individuals because of the numbers involved. There are too many prisoners, too few prison officers, and too little space to be able to do anything at all about it.

Mr Fletcher had been asked to give a lecture on the training needs of probation officers. Many have mentally ill people on their caseloads, for which they, like the prison officers, have had no training whatsoever. West Yorkshire Probation Service employs a specialist, the only initiative of its kind in the whole of the Probation Service. Probation Service officers are basically counsellors. They could presumably help to treat people better in some cases than psychiatrists, provided they received some kind of professional training. A mental health element should be introduced into probation training schedules by means of a post-qualification course. Those in the Probation Service who already have considerable experience in that particular area could be used to qualify and then gradually to train the rest.

Prison medical services at present are pretty poor. An extension of hospital facilities is clearly called for. In the prisons, the medical service tends to be used as part of the control system. The Prison Department buys in what medical service it needs from the regional health authority, but the prison doctor is accountable to the prison governor. Doctors have responsibility for health and safety conditions generally; one doctor recently closed the medical wing at Wandsworth. A prison doctor has the power to decree that certain parts of the prison are not in a fit state; he can indicate where lighting and ventilation are defective. But they often refrain from doing so.

Mr Fletcher said he could envisage the PMS being absorbed by the NHS, since it is beyond the power of the PMS to deal with the complex problem of the mentally ill offender.

It would be pointless to put people into community care if they were in need of psychiatric treatment. A better plan would be to have a system of probation combined with psychiatric care, if the mentally ill person can be persuaded to consent to undergo treatment. The ideal could well be a combination of both.

Mr Fletcher said that if called upon to suggest what steps could be taken to improve the whole question of mental offenders he would insist that any changes made on behalf of the mentally ill in prison should be brought within the criminal justice system as a whole, thus increasing awareness of the nature of mental illness throughout. This in turn would mean that the police would be discouraged from laying charges against a person who was mentally ill (where violence was not involved and there was no serious danger to the public); and the Crown Prosecution Service would be advised not to proceed with prosecution.

Police officers would need to be provided with information on the services for the mentally ill, such as addresses where advice can be obtained; local hospitals, probation offices, and so on. The health authority, in conjunction with all other relevant agencies, could produce such information. The police could advise the person to go to one of these services, thus ensuring he or she did not get into the prison system.

The Crown Prosecution Service could have a checklist to be used when deciding whether to proceed with the prosecution of a mentally ill person. It would be the duty of the Probation Service to bring to the notice of the court all relevant information as to the defendant's psychiatric condition, and, if the person is non-violent, to find a suitable community placement, such as, for example, a psychiatric hospital. The Department of Health, the Home Office, and the housing authorities would have to provide the resources between them.

Peter Thompson
Founder and Director, The Matthew Trust for Mental Patients and Victims of Crime

While books have been written by ex-prisoners and former patients of mental hospitals, only two such authors have gone on to work persistently for the benefit of inmates of such places, one being Peter Thompson, who spent four years in Broadmoor (1965–9), detained under Section 60 of the Mental Health Act 1959.

As I write I have in front of me an impressive document from The Matthew Trust, which Mr Thompson founded in 1976. It is headed *The Matthew Trust – A Report for the 1990s.* I select three passages in particular to quote:

> *Client Care:* grants made by The Matthew Trust have helped with Open University professional courses, the setting-up of small businesses, members of families visiting relatives in prisons and special hospitals, refurbishment of dilapidated accommodation, purchasing security alarms for victims, legal and independent medical, psychiatric (for mental health review tribunals) and social work services throughout the country.

> The Trust has concerned itself with the management of the treatment and disposal of patients in special hospitals and the mentally ill in prisons and at work, as well as with the media's attitude to the mentally disordered. Proposed and existing legislation affecting our client base has also been uppermost in the conduct of the Trust's activities, as well as the initiation of programmes of research and reform.

> Since 1971 Peter Thompson fought hard for patients in special hospitals to have legal aid to be represented at mental health review tribunals. In 1976 The Matthew Trust pursued the matter vigorously. Patients now have this facility. In 1968/69 Peter Thompson had had no legal aid for his mental health tribunal . . .

Since its inception, The Trust has given invaluable assistance – directly and indirectly – to some 1,500 former patients, prisoners, and victims of aggression, as well as to those who are socially disadvantaged. The Trust faces the stark fact that the mentally disordered and the mentally ill in prison are of little interest to business foundations and charitable trusts. Officially, such people, according to social workers reporting to The Trust, are treated by the Home Office and the Department of Health as 'undeserving'. On a yearly average, over the last few years, The Matthew Trust, for lack of funds, has turned down requests for individual grants exceeding the sum of £40,000 a year. Against this factor, sponsoring agencies, statutory and charitable, have approached The Trust for clients who have otherwise failed to qualify for statutory financial assistance.

Inspired by an ex-patient from Broadmoor who had no personal resources, The Matthew Trust emerges today as a fine example of what can be achieved by a passionate belief in a vital but always neglected cause. Peter Thompson is a highly articulate man who has written and spoken about mental health for the last 20 years. Nothing, however, that he has written or said has been more poignant than a sermon he gave on 27 October 1972 at the public school Tonbridge, three years after his release from Broadmoor. A few extracts are all there is room for here:

Can one be a mental offender and a Christian? That is a question many have asked since the publication of my book *Bound for Broadmoor*. I reply: 'Can a leper be a Christian?' In other words, is a mental offender any more responsible for his condition than a leper? Mental illness and leprosy are both diseases; one spoils the body, the other poisons the mind.

Having tasted of prison life and lived in Broadmoor, I sometimes wonder whether society today hankers after the forbidding code of 'an eye for an eye' and turns a blind eye to God's promise in Leviticus 26, when he says that if the people accept punishment for their iniquities, he will remember them. It seems to me that society condemns and forgets.

And then this, straight from his own experience:

Every crime committed by a mentally ill person is a two-fold tragedy, one for the person injured or offended against, and one for the offender. More often than not, the offender, before he or she commits the crime, has been crying out for help from a society too deaf to hear.

As he approached his conclusion, Peter Thompson laid himself bare before a seven-hundred-strong congregation:

I stand here today, a one-time mental offender, a danger to society, a social leper, following thirty years of mental illness that led me through the dark and ugly corridors of suicide attempts, depressions and paranoia. I lived with the socially damned, but came through these ordeals whole. Not because I was given preferential treatment, not because strings were pulled, but because I found in Broadmoor the personal love of our Lord, Jesus Christ – a love that put me on the road to believing that, whatever else, Christ cares for me.

Peter Thompson's childhood could hardly have been more horrifying. At the age of about three he and his sister were sent to a private home for children of broken families because his father was beating him. 'We were in an invidious position, my sister and I, when I was four years old and she was two. Twice we were medically diagnosed as suffering from malnutrition. We used to steal food because of hunger. Our punishment was to be locked up in a dark cellar for twelve hours or more. Rats could be heard scuttling across the coals.'

The woman in charge of him was having an affair with his father. When Peter Thompson complained to him, he was given a whipping from her and it was 'down to the cellar again'. After a three-year nightmare, he was eventually rescued by his mother. As he grew, he went through lengthy periods of unhappiness, suffering from deep depression leading to suicide bids, intense feelings of isolation, and paranoia. The story of his first connection with prisoners is one that I have recorded before, but it is well worth the re-telling:

In 1958, when he was a young man just starting out on his career, he was robbed by a man whom he later discovered had just been released from prison, after serving several years preventative detention. During these years the man had lost his home, family and job, and had received no help on his release. Although Peter Thompson wanted to drop the subsequent case, telling the police that he would give the man a home and provide for him, they refused. So Peter Thompson hired a lawyer to defend the man. The thief was given a light sentence, during which time Peter Thompson visited him in prison, where he was able to see for himself the lack of help given to men on their release, which gave rise to his deep concern for and interest in prisoners thereafter.

Peter Thompson was a critical out-patient in a hospital's psychiatric department, tormented by the despairing stories of others. He had been consulting the director-general of the Institute of Directors, who had been supporting and advising him. The director-general and the chairman of the House of Lords committees both suggested he should set up his own inquiry into the after-care of prisoners. Peter Thompson took this advice.

The inquiry was called The Pakenham/Thompson Committee. Peter Thompson pulled together a very strong body of people for the Committee, and its report paved the way for the establishment of a statutory inquiry into the problems of ex-offenders, and ultimately to the setting up of the National Association for the Care and Resettlement of Offenders (NACRO), the incorporation of an after-care service into the existing Probation Service, and the use of probation associates to establish contact with long-term prisoners prior to release.

'Rab' Butler (later Lord Butler), then Home Secretary, initially ignored the Pakenham/Thompson Committee's report until, in 1961, Peter Thompson persuaded Field-Marshal Lord Montgomery to make his maiden speech in the House of Lords on the main recommendations of the Committee. Lord Montgomery's speech attracted wide publicity. 'Rab' Butler immediately set up a statutory inquiry which took evidence from the Pakenham/Thompson Committee and, in its findings, embraced the Committee's central recommendations.

By 1964, however, many people close to Peter were having their fears confirmed that for many years he had been operating under overwhelming psychological difficulties. (About this time he told me he used to visit people in prisons since he found in them a sense of peace and security!) In 1965, after an attempt on his life and admission to a London hospital, on discharge he subsequently attacked three people he did not know, and was eventually admitted under Section 60 of the Mental Health Act 1959 as a patient to Broadmoor Hospital.

Peter would not now claim, I think, that this period in Broadmoor was unhelpful. The hospital gave him roots, a sense of stability, as well as stabilizing his mental and physical health. Above all, for the first time he felt himself to be part of a family who cared and who cast no scorn. However, he soon underwent a profound disillusionment: 'I had lived for those four years in a protected environment and had been led to regard my problem as one of mental illness, rather than criminality! . . . I thought I would be seen in that light by the wider community on my release . . . On the contrary, whereas the prisoner is regarded by many to have paid his debt to society for his crime, the ex-special hospital patient is looked upon by many in the outside world with continuing fear and suspicion, even by caring agencies.'

When discharged, the hospital authorities provided Peter with no special welfare support. His family and home had broken up while he was in Broadmoor. He set himself the task to improve the life of those released from special hospitals, but he never forgot the victims of crime, whether or not mental crime. The Matthew Trust has always cared not only for the mentally disordered, but also for the victims of violent crime:

> An offender should no longer be seen as a criminal reject of society, but as a casualty within society, a society that has morally pursued a dated course of retribution.

> The concept of admonishment allows for the offender to be given due regard in terms of his natural dignity. The offender is thereby not debased as a human being and is more receptive to a reformative process of reparation and rehabilitation.

Peter Thompson, quoted above, says that his view is the opposite of mine. There is ambiguity here. In my book *Punishment and the Punished* (1991), I have accepted the necessity of punishment as an important element in any society that we can foresee. I have accepted it on the assumption that the vast majority of those who break the law must be treated as responsible for their actions. Without such an assumption, I do not believe that law and order can be maintained. I speak without prejudice to the Divine influence which is not in this life disclosed to us.

But in the case of mental offenders, I accept a different assumption, which is itself accepted today in our public policy. I accept that in a special hospital like Rampton, for example, the inmate is treated not as a criminal, but as the patient. There is no question of blaming him and indeed a quarter or so of the patients in special hospitals have not been convicted.

In regard to mental offenders, therefore, I have no fundamental objections to Peter Thompson's approach, though I do not think that the word 'admonishment' conveys his full meaning. The blurred distinction between the concept of punishment and that of treatment has provoked me into attempting to explore the whole matter in the present book.

Today Peter Thompson has found more peace than he has expected to find in this life. It is this peace and stability which have enabled him to be, over the last 14 years, not only a successful businessman, but an untiring labourer on behalf of those suffering mental affliction.

Jerry Westall
The National Schizophrenia Fellowship

The further I made my way into the perplexing subject of mentally disordered offenders, the more I became aware that their treatment falls between two stools: the Home Office is responsible for the punishment of offenders, the Department of Health for the treatment of the sick. If the mentally ill are the Cinderellas of the social services, mentally disordered offenders are Cinderella's younger sister.

Jerry Westall is well-equipped to put the problem of mentally disordered offenders into a practical perspective. While working for The New Bridge for ex-prisoners, he brought about a big expansion of the service. Now a leading figure of the National Schizophrenia Fellowship, he is concerned with a large population of the mentally ill, including mentally disordered offenders. In discussion with me, he gave his top priority to the treatment at present – scandalous in his view – of the mentally ill on remand in prison. He insists that the immediate solution is the establishment of a number of psychiatric bail hostels. An extract from the evidence he gave to Lord Justice Woolf's committee brings this out forcibly:

Mr Westall:	What we are asking is for those people of no fixed abode to be sent on bail to a psychiatric bail hostel.
Judge Tumim:	Are you suggesting there is enough provision locally?
Mr Westall:	I am suggesting that people should not be going to prison if they have psychiatric problems on remand.
Judge Tumim:	Are there sufficient psychiatric bail hostels?
Mr Westall:	No. There are not, nothing like it. They should be developed rapidly. We are in the process of trying to . . .
Judge Tumim:	Yes, I understand that.
Mr Westall:	We are trying to establish a psychiatric bail hostel in Birmingham at the moment as a multi-agency

group with the Regional Forensic Psychiatric Service, the West Midland Probation Service and with the support of the Mental Health Foundation and others . . .

Judge Tumim: I follow that. But that does not solve the problem of today, does it, of the Prison Service?

Mr Westall: It will, if these places are established rapidly. We recognize that this is a pilot scheme. It should not take too long. It will cost a great deal less to establish this régime in these facilities than to carry on building more prisons.

Jerry Westall by no means confines his criticism to the treatment of remand prisoners. He insists there is a growing number of people going into the prison system with mental health problems. 'The psychiatric hospitals in this country have been reduced substantially from 1956, when there were 150,000 people in mental hospitals; there are now something like 50,000. In the next five years, 42 mental hospitals will be closing and at least 15,000 places will go.' He has no doubt that the alternative facilities will not be available.

In the last year that statistics were available, very many people were referred to the psychiatrists. If Mr Westall had his way, the closing down of mental hospitals would stop immediately and not be resumed until community care became a reality and not just a pious expression. Professor Wing (see page 56) has been advising the National Schizophrenia Fellowship for many years. Jerry Westall agrees with him that a sharp line must not be drawn between the hospitals and those who provide community care. Some of the present mental hospitals indeed should be the centre and focus of community care in the future.

On 7 November 1990, the National Schizophrenia Fellowship issued a press statement under the heading *Schizophrenia Call for Hospital Land Sale to Create New 'Haven Communities'*. The first paragraph read,

The National Schizophrenia Fellowship (NSF), Britain's leading mental health organization, today called on the government to turn some of the United Kingdom's large mental hospitals into 'haven communities' by selling off part of the land for residential or well-planned business use, and with the funds obtained building new, domestic style units.

An adequate provision of community care will not be a cheap option. But it is an indispensable requirement if any kind of justice is to be done to the mentally ill, including, of course, mental offenders. The sale of hospital land would play an invaluable part in answering the question: 'Where is the money to come from?' So would a cessation or restriction of the prison building programme.

Marjorie Wallace

Executive Director, Schizophrenia – A National Emergency (SANE)

Marjorie Wallace can fairly be described as the queen of campaigning journalists. She has more than once won awards as Campaigning Journalist of the Year, and recently spent a year as a Fellow of Nuffield College, Oxford, in campaigning journalism.

In her second *Guardian* lecture, *Campaign and be Damned*, she asked the question: 'And What Should a Campaigner be Fighting?' She answers it in this way:

> Over the past twenty years, I have been involved with dozens of campaigns from pollution, as in Seveso, to the exposure of demolition workers to asbestos. I have fought against our treatment of old people; warned of the waste of £3,000 million spent on concrete tower blocks which were so alien to human life that they had to be demolished ten years later; written about individual battles for awareness and compensation.

Since 1983, Marjorie, now a director of SANE, has done more than anyone to awaken the public to the tragedy of schizophrenia and the urgent need to mitigate its effects. Against that background I questioned her about the relationship between mental ill health, particularly schizophrenia, and breaking the law.

Lord Longford:	How far have you had dealings with the special problems of the mentally disordered? I assume that most of the people you have dealt with have not committed any crimes – but is there no question of the delinquents?
Marjorie Wallace:	Is there not a relationship between the community care policy and the large numbers of people now living on the streets, and the increased numbers who find themselves in prison? In the United States they have done far more research into this aspect. There, as in this

country, there are more people suffering from schizo-phrenia or manic depression in prison than in the public domain, or in mental hospitals. There has been a marked increase in the numbers of the mentally ill in prison, and the question is whether there is a direct link to the closure of the mental hospitals.

LL: What is your opinion?

MW: I do think there is a link, but it is difficult to prove. My view is that our research is lacking, apart from a recent study commissioned by the Home Office and con-ducted by Professor John Gunn in conjunction with the Maudsley Hospital [see page 50]. [The findings were published towards the end of 1991.] One in five of the prisoners interviewed had been suffering from serious mental illness.

LL: Many think the numbers are about 1,000. Do you go along with the approach that many in prison are in need of psychiatric treatment?

MW: Prison is serving as an asylum or sanctuary at the present time, because the medical profession no longer offers these facilities. Hospitals are either being closed altogether or run down, owing to shortage of staff. Low staff morale has led to many of the better trained leaving to set up their own 'second mortgage' homes for the mentally ill. I have known four or five such places where many patients have been restored to health and been able to go back home. Staff pick out the promising ones and offer them the opportunity to join the new set-up.

LL: Why do you feel there is a relationship between the numbers of people in prison and the closure of the mental hospitals?

MW: Because people with mental problems who at one time would have looked to the medical profession for help can no longer get into a mental or psychiatric hospital.

LL: What are you campaigning for now?

MW: We are getting more and more cases of people who have suffered a mental breakdown, are clearly very ill and are no longer accepted for treatment in hospital, but are being sent out to lodging houses, bed and breakfast accommodation or becoming homeless and living rough on the streets in a desperate state. They then commit a petty offence, have even been told to throw a brick through a shop window in order to get help by being arrested for criminal damage. At one time they would have been picked up by the police and taken to a psychiatric hospital for assessment, but now they are put in remand, and more often than not end up in prison. Because the need for care in the early stages is not being met, my conviction is that more people are becoming criminals who would otherwise never have done so.

LL: My own conclusion is that they should halt the closure of the large mental hospitals until alternatives are provided. Most people think we should have smaller units. Would you agree that Broadmoor should be liquidated? What would you put in its place?

MW: You should have smaller, more humane places with four or five people . . .

LL: Somewhat larger, surely. How would you treat mentally ill people who have not committed any crime?

MW: The philosophy was that large institutions should be demolished. Broadmoor is a self-contained city within a city, with its own hierarchy, its own rules and regulations. It should be replaced by a number of small special units. But the argument against this is that you get a fragmentation of expertise among staff. You run the risk of not being able to get enough qualified staff to go round. You lose your centres of excellence. The Broadmoor situation is a difficult one. Because it is run as a whole environment, it provides a secure haven for people who are seriously disturbed. A vast training scheme is called for before you can set up a whole lot of secure units or hospitals where 24-hour care can be provided.

You asked me what I am campaigning for at present. We campaign for mentally ill people, to ensure their care and treatment, whether offenders or not. There were terrible abuses in mental hospitals prior to the 1950s, before drugs were available – only padded cells and straitjackets. The humane concept of the old Victorian ideal of the lunatic asylum had become very distorted. Now the balance has swung too far the opposite way – the individual's right to freedom has been allowed to overshadow his right to care and treatment. The philosophy was that there was no need to contain people, so the voluntary system was introduced. The ideal of liberation took hold. Drugs were used and people given medication instead of being locked up. The civil liberties movement of the 1960s provided the seeds for the community care policy. A whole lot of States in America, appalled by the horrors of institutional care, which could and did breed mental illness, adopted a policy of freedom for the individual.

LL: Is the policy right? Can you provide care in the community?

MW: If you regard these people as being ill, what they need is expert, skilled treatment. If you regard them as suffering from a social condition, that is not illness. Mental illness cannot be explained away by saying that it is the result of poor social conditions or family upbringing.

LL: Is it correct to say that somebody is slightly schizophrenic?

MW: Yes. There is a spectrum. Take twins, for example. If one is diagnosed schizophrenic, there is only a 50

percent chance that both will be affected. Schizophrenia is an aggregate of symptoms.

LL: Assuming there are a lot of people who are slightly
schizoid, are you saying they are not ill enough to be in
hospital?

MW: People can also be labelled 'schizophrenia affected'.

LL: I am very keen on the idea that mentally disturbed
people in prison should be given much more treatment.
You are saying that people who are remotely schizophrenic should be packed off to hospital?

MW: No. This is where we are talking about community care.
If you look at current statistics, it costs £74 per day per
person for institutional care, but community care costs
only 29 pence a day.

LL: What would you do if you were dictator? If there were,
say, a reasonable increase in the resources available?

MW: If I were a dictator I would look at two things. First, the
cost of providing the kind of care needed, and I would
look at the ideologies which led to the concept that
physical freedom was paramount over families' rights,
or someone's rights to care and treatment. One symptom is that the person is irrational – their illness does not
give them a choice; they are prisoners of their illness. Let
us look at freeing them from their illness. It is no good
giving people freedom and community care if you are
not actually tackling the illness.

    The first thing you have to do is to put a lot of
resources into tackling the illnesses themselves, do more
research. Prevent people from falling ill. I would take
the priority that has been given to cancer research over
the last two years and would give the same degree of
priority of research to mental problems, to pinpoint the
causes. Schizophrenia conveys a certain dignity – it is
a label. Find the cause and give the treatment called for.

My second point would be: forget the ideology of liberty and ensure that people can receive the care and treatment they need. You have to be able to provide asylum or sanctuary in the old sense of the word. It is no good saying that a person suffering a breakdown can see a consultant in three months' time.

LL: But if they don't want to go to hospital, what would you do about it?

MW: There are a lot of cases which will remain difficult to cope with. There are many people needing help who are being pushed about because there is nothing suitable available for them.

LL: How could the prime minister, say, halt the closures? Take a particular area, for example the south-east. Hellingly Hospital had 1,400 beds at one time for mental cases and was supposed to take 1,000 patients. When I last went there they were down to 100 and would soon be closed altogether. I asked what was being done about the patients. It came out that 200 were being looked after in small units, but that was all. The government has to decide – it does mean more money.

MW: If you talk to the chairmen of the regional health authorities they all say they have not got the facilities. What is happening in the psychiatric field is that everybody is becoming demoralized, lacking hope. That is why we campaign – to help. Psychiatrists regard themselves as professionals; they do not campaign.

LL: Who are you trying to convince as a campaigner? Is it the ministers?

MW: My three aims are, first, to provide a massive influx of resources into what people need and giving illness the benefit of the doubt – not hiding under the cloak of general social problems. A lot of money must be invested into building up alternative care.

Second, you have to make sure the regional authorities have the alternative facilities available before being allowed to close the hospitals. A number of bodies have set up hospital/hostels, about 12 altogether in this country, as an outcome of research. These are a replacement for the sort of care you could expect to receive if really ill and needing to go to a psychiatric hospital.

LL: Do you agree that community care is hard to arrange?

MW: We have gone over the top on civil liberties and now have to redress the balance. Families should be consulted far more often, and given support, which is often lacking now. This has got to be done – get under control the philosophy of the social workers. The family must be involved once again.

My third point I see as very important: you are not going to achieve any of these objectives until the public are made aware of mental illness, until mental illness is treated more openly and not regarded as something to be ashamed of. The stigma should be removed, otherwise no real progress is possible. My major campaign at present is to increase awareness.

LL: Do you know anybody at present who admits to having a schizophrenic child?

MW: Families do not readily admit to this problem. This is what makes campaigning so difficult. Many people who commit suicide are schizophrenics, but the cause is rarely admitted as such.

Jane Branston
Effra House

For 17 years, day in and day out, Jane Branston has run Effra House, which was set up by Professor John Gunn of the Maudsley Hospital in 1974 under the auspices of the Royal London Aid Society, to provide accommodation and support for homeless epileptic ex-offenders aged 18–65.

In July 1980 the Effra Trust became an independent charity working in partnership with the London and Quadrant Housing Trust. The Trust expanded its brief to provide care for ex-offenders with other forms of illness or disability. There are two houses, and together with a two-bedroomed training flat in Rattray Road, they have a total of 17 beds available. A further four single bed units are allocated each year by Lambeth Housing for men who are ready to live on their own in the community. Residents are referred to Effra House from many sources, including the Probation Service, the Prison and Social Services, as well as the resettlement units. The decision to accept a man is made in consultation with the management committee, after discussion with the other residents, whose feelings are taken into consideration.

The crucial test is that of a man's apparent motivation and willingness to fit in with other residents. Most residents attend Professor Gunn's clinic at the Maudsley Hospital. It has never been easy for residents to find employment, and today the prospect of obtaining regular work is more than ever difficult. A programme of activities of an educational and recreational nature is provided. The houses are run on relaxed and informal lines, as experience has taught that an important element in the control of epilepsy and other disorders is the elimination of as much tension as possible.

The first word that comes to Jane Branston's lips when you ask about her objective is 'asylum'. (This, incidentally, was the word which was emphasized to me by the director of medical services at Rampton.) A synonym, I suppose, would be 'home'. I put it to her that what was needed was a whole lot of Effra Houses. She did not dissent. It would not be difficult, given the resources, to multiply Effra House; very much harder to multiply Jane Branston.

She told me that she owed everything to the teaching and inspiration of Professor Gunn; it would be surprising if her approach to the national problem was not similar to his. She shares his enthusiasm for regional secure units, as well as a desire to see mental health facilities much expanded, the emphasis being on small units rather than large institutions. She returned more than once to the need for rescuing many mentally afflicted people from the criminal justice system before it was too late.

I have visited Effra House more than once and come away with a new sense of hopefulness about what could be done for mentally disturbed offenders. The spirit of partnership between helpers and the helped, always under firm leadership, is very inspiring. But it will not be achieved to the extent achieved in Effra House without much dedication and much love.

The National Association for the Care and Resettlement of Offenders (NACRO)

On 23 December 1990 NACRO produced *The Imprisonment of Mentally Disturbed Offenders*, a non-judgmental document that begins by quoting the recent Home Office document called *The Sentence of the Court*, which clearly implies that we are sending too many mentally disturbed offenders to prison (see page 21). The NACRO document suffers, as we all do in these discussions, from an ambiguity in the use of terms. When it deals with mentally disordered prisoners, it provides statistics which relate to several different categories of person. During the year 1989–90, over 16,000 prisoners were referred to psychiatrists – 38 percent more than in 1987–88, and during a period when the prison population as a whole slightly decreased.

The exact number of mentally disordered prisoners is unknown. The only information available comes from a number of prison surveys. But can we say that *everyone* referred to a psychiatrist is mentally disturbed? A different test is applied to another quotation: 'Some disturbed prisoners suffer from disorders which fall within the criteria of the Mental Health Act 1983 for compulsory detention in hospital. On 31 March 1990 there were 290 such people in prison. It can be safely assumed that this figure of 290 is a gross underestimate.' But even if we say that, for example, the figure of 1,000 would be nearer the mark, it in no way compares with the 16,000 prisoners who were referred to psychiatrists in 1989–90.

The issue is of importance on the theoretical side. If we say that those responsible for the crime should be punished, but that those who are mentally sick should be treated as patients, where do we draw the line?

NACRO describes the existing position for mentally disturbed prisoners in the prison system. They mention the fact that one-third of prisoners who commit suicide have been treated as in-patients prior to imprisonment, and a large number have been treated as out-patients. They leave a clear implication that the present provision in the prison system is extremely inadequate. They describe at length the provision outside prison and the methods of disposal open to the courts. They conclude that the courts' options are limited by a lack of hospital provision. NACRO also comment sharply on the number of defendants remanded in custody who eventually receive a hospital order.

NACRO addressed themselves carefully to the problem of 'diverting mentally disturbed offenders from the criminal justice system . . . the difficulties that courts have in finding appropriate places for many disturbed offenders may be overcome in part by the provision of more hostels and day care facilities'.

They argue, however,

> . . . even within existing resources it is contended that more can be done to divert mentally disturbed offenders from the criminal justice system. Because no single agency has overall responsibility for them, mentally disturbed offenders may be 'passed' from one agency to another instead of getting the care and support they need. By working more closely together, criminal justice agencies, local housing, health and social services can help ensure that mentally disturbed offenders get the treatment they need and that better use is made of finite resources.

They quote at some length the guidance given by the Home Office which should result in more transfers from the courts to hospital. Whether it does or not remains to be seen.

There is finally a heading 'Mentally Disturbed People and Community Care':

> In addition to the need for additional appropriate hospital places and other community provision for mentally disturbed offenders, it is widely agreed that there is a need for extra community provision for people discharged from psychiatric hospitals. [NACRO quote what they call] evidence to support the view that there is a lack of community support.'

The last passage of the NACRO report is one to dwell on: 'An adequately resourced and carefully implemented community care programme may help prevent the imprisonment of mentally disturbed people.'

Chris Tchaikovsky
Founder and Director, Women in Prison

Chris Tchaikovsky is the founder and the life and soul of the Women in Prison Movement. Coming from a wealthy family, she took to international crime at the age of 17 and practised it with no small success for 13 years. Finally she was caught and sent to prison. On emerging she took a good degree, and went on to perform a remarkable service to women in prison and to prisoners generally.

Chris Tchaikovsky had sent me a good deal of material in advance, much of it relating to the notorious C1 unit at Holloway Prison, which had been the subject of widespread and vehement criticism in 1984 and subsequently. Most of the prisoners in C1, the unit for the highly disturbed, are on remand for psychiatric assessment. Chris acknowledged that there have been a lot of improvements lately: fewer women are placed on report and punished; the atmosphere is less tense; more women are out of their cells for longer periods; more women are in the skills training unit. There has not, however, been adequate change in the staff composition since 1984.

The downside is that C1 is still claustrophobic and squalid, with cockroaches. The unit takes 35 women. Some of them are locked up alone in their cells for twenty-three hours a day. There are long periods of isolation. Chris has no doubt that C1 should be closed.

She also thinks that the Mental Health Act of 1983 should be amended. Prisons should no longer be described as a 'place of safety'. The death rate of the mentally disturbed group revealed that 'If one is a danger to oneself or a danger to others, one should be assessed by an NHS psychiatrist.' She laid much stress on the psychiatrist being an NHS psychiatrist: 'If necessary, one should be transferred to a secure unit in a mental hospital, or a regional secure unit. The large special hospitals such as Broadmoor and Rampton should be closed. There should be *small* units for people who need intensive support and care.' She agreed that tender loving care was much more likely in small units.

Chris Tchaikovsky has an undying objection to prisons:

Prisons can never be anything other than prisons. One cannot graft a therapeutic regime on to a punitive one. No more psychiatric units should be created in prisons. Indeed, there should not be psychiatric units in prisons at all. Disordered people, including sex offenders, should be in hospital . . . Prisons exacerbate mental disorder. Prison does not work and never will. It is no deterrent for anything.

One is bound to ask what she would do with the vast majority of offenders who could not be described as mentally disordered.

Chris has a strong belief in the possibility of reforming offenders through education and, above all, by *bonding* – the establishment of a loving relationship between the offender and another human being. She argued, 'People should talk to a therapist they trust and learn about themselves. Group therapy or one-to-one therapy, plus interactions with ordinary people in the community, is the right answer.' (Even though psychiatrists are not always helpful.) A therapeutic or educational environment should be provided. 'Dangerous criminals or sex offenders should not be studied like specimens.'

She is severely critical of community care as now practised. It would, she says, be truer to call it 'cruelty in the community'. She is, however, full of praise for the Barnet Crisis Intervention team attached to Barnet General Hospital and feels there should be a nation-wide scheme of this kind, but ideally not attached to hospitals. The psychiatric social workers involved are lay people with common sense. The police have no desire to keep mentally disordered people in their cells. Faced with such people, they call on the psychiatric social workers. If the assessment is that they are disordered, 'they are found a bed in an interim or regional secure unit. If they are not disordered and it is a serious crime, they go through the criminal justice system.' Chris Tchaikovsky summed it up: 'This scheme would work more cheaply than keeping people in prison.'

I asked her whether she had anything special to say about the treatment of women. She made the rather surprising pronouncement that:

The excessive psychiatrication of women should cease. If a woman rather than a man commits arson, then she is 'depressed'. This erodes her individual responsibility. 'Boys will be boys', but women are turned into slaves and stopped from being full human beings. Men continue to think that women are 'addled', especially once a month.

I am bound to say that I find myself lost. At one moment Chris seemed to be saying that offenders who are mentally disordered should be treated in a different way from normal prisoners. They should not be sent to prison, they should go to hospital. But she now seems to be saying that women are more likely to be held to be mentally disordered than men, and that that works out to their disadvantage. However, no one doubts that she has been of enormous service to many women in distress.

Dr N. A. Hindson
Chief Medical Officer, Holloway Prison

Dr Hindson, the Chief Medical Officer of Holloway Prison, was at one time in charge of C1, the unit reserved for disturbed prisoners mostly on remand, and which had earned a most unenviable reputation before he came on the scene. Dr Hindson has since become the Chief Medical Officer of the whole prison, but continues to take a special interest in C1.

The comparison that kept coming into my mind was with C Wing, Parkhurst. There also are grouped disturbed prisoners, although this includes some who are considered the most dangerous in the prison system. There are, however, marked differences between the two prisons, apart from the fact that the men in Parkhurst are a good deal more dangerous than the disturbed women in C1. In C Wing, Parkhurst, there are 32 staff to 18 prisoners. In C1, Holloway, there are 22 staff to a maximum of 41 prisoners (not usually achieved). In Parkhurst, the governor of the unit and some of the other members of the staff have had the training of nursing officers. In Holloway, 17 of the 22 are trained nurses, which of course implies a much longer training. The senior nursing officers at Holloway have had training and possess a mental health qualification. (The nursing officers I have talked to in C Wing, Parkhurst, are as deeply imbued with what I would call the nursing philosophy as the nurses in charge at Holloway.) The five remaining members of the staff at Holloway include a doctor with a psychiatric background, two probation officers and two security staff, in other words, prison officers.

In spite of a well-justified sense of achievement, Dr Hindson does not consider the set-up in C1 ideal. At the present time, 75 percent of the patients are on remand, and 25 percent are convicted. He would like to see the convicted prisoners transferred to a place like Grendon, where they could be handled as a relatively long-term problem. The remand prisoners are awaiting assessment, which is provided partly by three consultant psychiatrists who visit weekly.

The Chief Medical Officer thinks it would be fatal to transfer the 25 percent convicted prisoners to the main prison. They would be utterly vulnerable, and in some cases destructive. I spoke to a young woman who has been in and out of Holloway several times; she is regarded as a suicide risk and needs very specialized treatment. I should mention that since 1985 there have been no suicides in C1, Holloway – a remarkable improvement on previous years.

Dr Hindson appears to prefer pragmatism to ideology, considering always the particular interest of the prisoner being dealt with. He entirely approves of efforts to make sure that psychiatrists are attached to the courts to make right assessments possible; he ridiculed the idea propounded by the government that there are not enough psychiatrists available.

I came away wondering whether the nursing principles so successful in Holloway and in a limited sense in C Wing, Parkhurst, could not be applied more widely in the prison service. Apparently Holloway's C Wing requires only two security officers because the nurses appear to manage satisfactorily with a month's training before taking on the work.

Before I left, I asked Dr Hindson for his comments on a document given to me by Women in Prison. This is a summary of what they call 'A Typical Day on C1 Unit' and includes an impression of that unit as it appears to a prisoner recently released. Although no individual could be fully representative, one has to say at once that this prisoner was very unhappy in C1. What saddens me in particular is that she found the nurses uncaring. She alleges that before the prison officers' strike in 1988, which apparently brought improvement, she was locked in for 23 hours a day. On one occasion she alleges that she was locked in her cell for seven days' solitary confinement as a punishment without adjudication.

When shown the foregoing, Dr Hindson commented:

Can I say that the regime on the unit was not 23 hours a day locked in prior to the prison officers' strike of 1988, but it is true that the amount of time unlocked was not as great as the typical day (from breakfast at 7.45a.m. to supper at 7p.m.). Since April 1986, it has been the practice not to place mentally disordered women before the governor for adjudication, so that the woman is locked in as punishment, but for clinical reasons for observation, assessment, and control. Such seclusion is reviewed on a daily basis. I do not know the individual who has spoken to you, but I can only think of six occasions in the last five years and four months when a patient has remained locked in under seclusion for as long as a week, because of concern about the patient's mental state and/or behaviour. On all occasions this has been due to incidents of serious assaults upon staff or fellow patients. As you can see, such instances are fortunately rare.

III Authorities on Sex Offenders

Professor Donald West
Professor Emeritus of Clinical Criminology, University of Cambridge Institute of Criminology

I asked Professor West whether a mentally disordered person would be called a psychopath if he could be helped by psychiatric treatment. He replied that many people displaying deviant behaviour could be helped by a psychiatric form of treatment known as behaviour modification, which does not necessarily involve a psychiatrist. The difficulty is that prisoners are often not recognized as mental cases and languish in prison lacking treatment.

Individuals who are unable to restrain themselves and are so uncontrolled as to be highly antisocial, doing damage to others, are then called psychopaths. There is a difference, for example, between paedophiles who do not do any harm and the murderous types. There are others who engage in incestuous activities and do not do anything outside the home.

If a man is only interested in immature children, this is something different from the normal and he can be helped to change – people's sexual drive can be changed. It is not easy to draw a line between those who are likely to respond to treatment and those who are not. There is a big difference between those who are primarily and immaturely attracted to children and those who use children for lack of an adult; others may only start offending with age, or on becoming widowers or after drinking alcohol; still others offend through general inadequacy and the failure to relate to others. The latter are usually the mentally impaired who are not accepted by adults but who are often accepted quite readily by children. All of these types are different from those who have a fixation.

With regard to mental offenders, Professor West pointed out, the problem is that the law tries to draw sharp distinctions, whereas nature does not. More people should be recognized as requiring help and this applied particularly to sex offenders. Another group are the substance abusers – drug and alcohol addicts. They may not be a problem in prison, but on release do need specialized help, primarily of a medical nature which could involve psychiatry.

Forensic psychiatrists hardly existed in the 1960s, Professor West went on to tell me, and there are still nothing like enough of them to serve magistrates' courts around the country. They tend to be centred in hospitals and otherwise thinly spread elsewhere. There is a need for hospital facilities to deal with the different types of problem. Facilities for dealing with alcohol and drug abuse problems are limited, and there are fewer facilities still for dealing with sexual problems. It is largely a matter of the health service developing facilities of a forensic psychiatric nature. Forensic psychiatrists are supposed to be, as it were, engaged with the law and attending to very serious cases. The paedophile, on the other hand, needs somebody capable of assessing the problem and recommending the appropriate treatment. What is required are units similar to the Gracewell Clinic in Birmingham (dependant at present on private funding, while trying unsuccessfully to obtain National Health Service support). Such units should be based in mental hospitals, supported by the health service, and staffed by psychologists, psychiatrists, and therapists.

As far as sex offenders are concerned, Professor West would like to see special units attached to hospitals. The lack of suitable facilities for the assessment and treatment of serious sex offenders could be met by such special units. In the United States, for example, the treatment of recidivist sex offenders has proved effective by committing them under a 'sexual psychopath' law for hospital assessment and, if found suitable, for subsequent hospital-based treatment in lieu of imprisonment. Their subsequent graded release into the community under supervision is governed by judicial review.

Professor West considered that it was necessary to develop specialized units under psychiatric control within the prison service itself. Those offenders who in the public interest have got to be imprisoned are entitled to the same treatment as if they were outside. A clear distinction between training and treatment in cases of personality disorder is required. Ideally such treatment is a form of social training. With problems of drug addiction and sexual disorders the kind of training is different, because the difficulty may arise from the lack of work discipline or of any skill.

In reply to the question as to what is being done in prison to help drug addicts and alcoholics, and whether he thought that the Mental Health Act 1983 should be altered to exclude this type of offence, Professor West replied that he was not so much concerned with the law as with the practice. He would like to see the individualization of sentencing – looking at the offender as well as the offence, instead of having a fixed tariff. It was a question of whether the sentence was looked at purely from a punitive angle or as a mechanism of social control. In the latter case, the individual had to be taken into account. Punishment is a necessary agent of control, but should be used with discretion. Judging by the size of the prison population and the length of sentences, we are unnecessarily punitive in this country, he felt.

Graham Willis
Co-ordinator, St Gabriel's Family Centre, Brighton

Mr Willis works under the auspices of the Church of England Children's Society, the Probation and Social and Health Services. He is carrying out a risk assessment and group treatment programme for men and adolescents who sexually abuse children. The aim is to develop a constructive response and forms of intervention for perpetrators of child abuse, to prevent the occurrence or repetition of child sexual abuse and reduce the damaging effects on children and their families.

Referrals are made from the Probation and Social Services, and the offender must have been through the courts, or be otherwise mandated to the group. The treatment programme is designed to serve as a possible alternative to custody. It provides a 'rigorous and confrontative response' to offending. It makes significant demands of time, energy, and commitment on the offender, and contributes to the 'active monitoring and supervision' of his behaviour.

Family centres began to be set up some 20 years ago, working with families and children together. Mr Willis explained that he had been a social worker for 20 years and for the last ten had been mainly concerned with child abuse and child sexual abuse. He worked at first with children and their families, but more recently with men who sexually abuse children, with a view to trying to prevent them from re-offending.

In reply to a question as to whether the men all came under the heading of paedophiles, Mr Willis replied that it was debatable. There were a number of definitions of a paedophile – somebody who is sexually attracted to children, somebody who acted out sexual attraction, and so on. For instance, he had recently seen a man who admitted to being attracted by little boys in short trousers, who had for many years been a cubmaster, in order to act out his sexual fantasies with them. He had also abused his own son, stepson and step-daughter, as well as having been very active in getting hold of small boys in general.

Some paedophiles concentrate on boys, but there is quite a lot of cross-over with the sexes. This is different from the man who has been married for ten or twelve years and who has not shown any particular interest in other children, but has abused his daughter when she is ten years old. It is debatable as to whether such a man is a paedophile or not. Some authorities distinguish between two kinds of paedophile: the fixated, who is sexually attracted primarily to children; and the regressed, the person who does not seem to have primary sexual interest in children, but at any time in his life when he comes under stress chooses to act against children.

In response to the question as to whether the behaviour is always hostile – one assumes the child is reluctant – Mr Willis said the child does not give consent. The man, however, would not see his behaviour as hostile, but would see it more as a way of showing love.

Men in a group meet once a week to discuss their problems with him. They look at the distorted thinking giving rise to their behaviour. These men, in the view of Mr Willis, are not mentally ill. Their distortion is fuelled by their belief that it is all right to have sex with children; they will say that the child wanted them to do it.

Mr Willis gave some examples of 'distortion'. For example, in a recent group he gave the men a list of rationalizations and asked them to tick those they used to justify their behaviour. They are able to stand outside their behaviour; they can see that they use such rationalizations. One man said: 'I convince myself that it is my way of showing affection.'

In many cases, the development of such men from childhood has actually predisposed them in some way to use this particular method of acting out their fantasies. But it is never a simple matter. Many people have had a bad upbringing and yet have turned out to be good citizens and vice versa. Men who commit incest, for example, often have had less than satisfactory relationships with their fathers. Socially, paedophiles come from all types of backgrounds, so poverty is not necessarily a factor. A considerable number have been exposed to physical abuse, a significant proportion to sexual abuse and/or inappropriate sexual behaviour within the family system.

Mr Willis explained that the regressed paedophile is somebody who reacts to the particular situation in which he finds himself. He stated unequivocally that every man he had worked with had deliberately chosen to abuse. They had thought about it and had then acted it out. Most men can be sexually aroused by fully developed young girls. The issue is whether they act it out or not. Sexual abuse is basically an abuse of power. The men he worked with have had relations with children of from five to fifteen years of age, but some had abused babies, the youngest having been just three years old. A man has control over a child, can make it masturbate him, have intercourse and buggery, even have oral sex – but this is mostly with very young children.

Not everybody would wish to work in a group; some would not wish to disclose themselves. But Mr Willis has found the group method more effective than one-to-one working, indeed more powerful. The men know who is 'conning' himself; they understand each other, accuse each other.

When I asked Mr Willis whether paedophiles should be punished or viewed as sick, he replied that he saw sex abuse as a crime. Crimes invoke consequences for which there is a price to pay. Some men do need to go to prison – prison reflects the seriousness of what they have done and in the short term protects other children, signalling at the same time to victims that this man is the one who has done wrong. It relieves the child of any feeling of guilt. The man is the one to blame; the child can feel that he was in some way responsible, and it has to be made quite clear that the man is the guilty one. This is particularly important when the man has shown the child more affection than the child is getting within the family, and/or if the abuse occurs within the context of genuine affection.

Mr Willis was of the opinion that some men would benefit from treatment from the start and need not go to prison. Others should go to prison because there is no other way of bringing home to them the seriousness of what they have done. Such men should get treatment in prison, but the problem there is that it is often short-term, given in an unreal atmosphere. There is also the problem that prison reinforces the distortion. Prison is a society in which men justify their actions to one another. Sex offenders swap anecdotes. In prison they feel more like victims themselves, and this bolsters them up and they lose sight of the wrong they have done. This is one of the drawbacks of custodial sentencing.

Mr Willis would like to see shorter sentences and longer periods of parole under supervision. I pointed out that violent offenders and sex offenders seem likely under present thinking to be in prison

longer. He would like to see more suspended sentences, which can
be acted upon if the men do not come for treatment. It works in the
United States. In this country they have to re-offend before it is acted
upon, so suspended sentences do not necessarily help his work.

I raised the question as to the possibilities of treatment, bearing in
mind that many paedophiles were recidivists. Is it possible to effect
cures? Mr Willis found it difficult to make any claims, inasmuch as
his work is quite new. One study of a large number of treatment
programmes found that on balance treatment was more effective
than doing nothing at all. The most definitive research shows that
certain types of treatment programme may be effective. But it is not
possible to change people's sexual arousal; you can only promote
control. As long as the men are involved in treatment, they are
reminded of the consequences – which means that treatment should
be for life, in the same way as for alcoholics. Once a sex offender,
always potentially a sex offender.

Ray Wyre
The Gracewell Clinic, Birmingham

Ray Wyre is mentioned with admiration by all those concerned with sex offenders and their problems. The Gracewell Clinic, Birmingham, we are told, 'is the first residential clinic of its kind. It runs the treatment and control programme pioneered by Ray Wyre. He developed this programme over a seven-year period in his work in prison, and subsequently in his clinic at St James' Hospital, Portsmouth.'

The Gracewell Clinic provides full-time, residential treatment for sex offenders who need intensive therapy in order to gain control of their behaviour. The clinic caters to 21 inmates (18 at the time of my visit) overseen by 15 staff. They are in principle there for a year and their residence is made a condition of probation. Their ages run from 25 to 70. I met six of them aged between 30 and 60.

While there is considerable supervision in the sense that the inmates cannot leave the clinic unaccompanied, they all agreed there is a whole world of difference between life there and life in prison. They clearly enjoyed a real sense of freedom in the clinic. Above all, they feel they are understood and treated as human beings. One fine-looking man in early middle age told me that he was married with three children, but had developed this irresistible urge to have sex with boys. (His sons were standing by him, but not so, I gathered, his wife; indeed he hoped to marry another lady.) Another, older man said that for 30 years he had entertained boys in his house and, he claimed, made them happy. He asked me how I would feel if I woke up one day and found that his form of love-life was the norm, and mine was prohibited. He did not find my answer convincing.

The clinic has only been open for two years and has won an excellent reputation. Professor Donald West (see page 96) reached this conclusion in *The Times*:

The English prison culture that persecutes men known to have committed sex offences is inimical to co-operation in treatment requiring honest self-revelation . . . The consequent necessity for segregation could be used to create centres for realistic treatment

... Constructive discussions of offending and its consequences, and of the thought processes that have permitted men to commit sex crimes, such as now take place at centres like the Gracewell Clinic, could then be held before men are released.

Gracewell is staffed by a multidisciplinary team of professionals experienced in working with problems of sexual abuse. I asked Mr Wyre whether they used any of the best-known models of treatment. He said they were eclectic: they drew on any method that was likely to be fruitful in an individual case. Drugs are not ruled out, but are not a main feature of the treatment. The official brochure says:

> If the habits and beliefs of a life-time are to be changed, specialized long-term intensive therapy is necessary. . . . If the risk of re-offending is to be reduced, treatment must be focused on the attitudes and beliefs that legitimize offending. . . . Offenders build whole armouries of denial for the protection of those distorted beliefs and perceptions which allow them to continue offending, without hearing that they are doing something wrong. . . . Treatment must also focus on the sexual arousal system and behaviour pattern which has been conditioned around offending itself.

Again and again it was emphasized to me that 'behavioural techniques can be effective in controlling deviant sexual fantasies'. Offenders, however, have no reason to use them if they believe their offending does no harm. Ray Wyre seems to feel that while one-to-one therapy is necessary, group therapy can be still more effective. From my talk with the inmates, I found them perfectly ready to talk freely with one another about their problems. Mr Wyre did not regard the inmates of the Gracewell Clinic, or sex offenders generally, as mental cases, although he agreed that someone mentally disordered could become a sex offender.

IV The House of Lords

Lord Ennals of Norwich
Former Secretary of State for Social Services

Lord Ennals began by referring to a recent Home Office report suggesting that prison medical services should no longer be the responsibility of the Home Office but that of the NHS on the grounds of their present highly unsatisfactory condition. He himself would welcome such a move. It was an issue to which his attention had been drawn as chairman of MIND, particularly during the 1980s.

He had become even more aware of the problem as secretary of state for health, but not perhaps to the degree which he should have done, although he did appreciate its significance as far as Broadmoor and other special hospitals were concerned. It has to be recognized that there are some psychiatric cases which call for secure conditions. But secure institutions must provide adequate treatment for their inmates. There is no provision at all in the community for these cases who need the protection of some form of asylum, provided it is not of an institutional type.

Lord Ennals accepts that the National Schizophrenia Fellowship has been making strenuous efforts to stop the rundown of long-stay hospitals, a rundown with which he does not agree. His view is that this policy should be balanced by provision in the community of small units. As secretary of state for health 14 years ago he had discussed this question with the Fellowship, but had not got as far as actually closing any hospitals. Numbers in long-stay hospitals were even then being steadily reduced, while alternative provision in the community was being steadily increased. To close down the hospitals without making alternative provision available was a crime. The government had announced the programme of community care, but left open the question as to whether it was the responsibility of the health authorities or that of the local authorities.

Lord Ennals had proposed they should proceed without delay on the community care part of the recent bill and postpone for at least two years the closing down of hospitals. In the event the government did exactly the opposite. There had been strong opposition in both Houses of Parliament against most of the proposals for the reform of the National Health Service, but the proposal for bringing community care into the hands of local authorities was strongly favoured, provided the money was available. To be fair to the bill, it was not just a matter of leaving it to the local authority; they were to have the major responsibility to do it through voluntary organizations and such like. The local authorities had to satisfy themselves that the provision was adequate.

Over the years, community care will become easier. It became difficult because the closure of large psychiatric hospitals removed a source of local treatment at a time when treatment was becoming more and more community based. There is a nucleus of patients whose interests are not served by community care. They need protection, but not of an institutional nature. This is best done by having a limited number of smaller hospitals to which they could be transferred. He would not like to put a figure to it.

In the NHS and Community Care Bill, the government decided to end the policy whereby local authorities could appoint representatives to the health authorities. It is a great mistake. It is now businessmen who will be running the health service, and good relations between the health authority and the local authority are going to become even more important in future. These management men are the people who cut the money down. There is a role for such people to see that money is effectively spent. Lord Ennals is in favour of cash limits for the health authorities, but there is an essential need for the closest possible co-ordination between the health and local authorities – a need which the government has hitherto neglected.

As far as mental offenders are concerned, the question is, who should make provision for them? Lord Ennals considered it to be the health service which should have responsibility for their physical and mental health. If offenders are going to be transferred from prison for more appropriate treatment elsewhere, funds would have to be transferred from one authority to another.

Lord Ennals agreed with Professor Gunn (see page 48) that the Mental Health Act of 1983 did not need to be amended. If adequate provision were made in the health service, there would be less opposition to accepting mental offenders in hospitals. It is argued that the Mental Health Act is often used to prevent prisoners from being accepted by hospitals, on the grounds that if a patient is not treatable then he should have no claims to a hospital's resources. But people's mental state is always changing, and it can take a long time to form an opinion. Any such argument is completely unacceptable in a civilized society.

Baroness Faithfull of Wolvercote
President, the National Children's Bureau; Former Director of Social Services, Oxford

Lady Faithfull and I agree that people with mental disorder are a severe test for the penal system:

> They are difficult to cope with. Other prisoners are frightened of them. Prison staff are not trained to deal with them. They are unable to treat them differently from other inmates, although they recognize that they are in fact different. If they are assessed as psychopaths, the judge can make an order for them to go to a mental hospital, assuming that the hospital is ready to take them. If not, judges have no option but to send them to prison.

At our interview, I wondered whether the existing law should be altered. Lady Faithfull replied that it was no good altering the law unless the necessary facilities were available. She did, however, agree that the law should be altered, but not until then. What she felt was important, and indeed found distressing, was that the Butler Report had made the need for more facilities quite clear, but nothing had been done except in the Oxford area, where three regional secure units had been set up.

The size and scope of these units have provoked considerable debate. Doctors favoured a large central regional unit, but she thought that several small places would be more suitable, because the men could be located nearer to their families. She did, however, come to realize later that this would have proved impracticable from a staffing point of view, and more costly. She had not altogether lost the argument in the end, because three separate units had emerged.

I mentioned that Dr Bullard (see page 43) was of the opinion that larger regional secure units ought to be able to accommodate longer-stay people. Lady Faithfull explained that she had been doubtful, because men are more easily coped with if they can see their families, but had given way to some extent to get something done. She pointed out, however, that only those who had worked in a prison could be aware of the degree of disturbance which the mentally disordered cause to other prisoners.

I referred to another very important suggestion she had made in her speech in my debate on Mental Offenders in 1988. She had thought that lesser offenders could be farmed out to bodies like the Church Army or the Salvation Army. She had gone into that aspect thoroughly. In Oxford there was a Church Army hostel which was badly run. Mentally inadequate people were being housed there and it was considered locally that the place should be closed. She helped to set up a committee and eventually, aided by funds from the Church Army and the ministry, a new hostel was opened. Although intended to be for the homeless, it has become almost a wing of the mental hospital. She is convinced that it has helped to prevent many of the men from getting into further trouble. The Church Army and the Salvation Army are in her view the most effective bodies in dealing with really difficult people. Many at present in prison could well be dealt with in these hostels.

I wondered how that would work. Could thieves be sent there, for example, or violent cases? Lady Faithfull did not think so – only the mentally inadequate and schizophrenics. If the men had been charged and the Church Army willing to accept them, the court would issue a probation order with a condition of residence. If they broke this, they would have to go to prison. In most cases, however, they proved to be fairly orderly people.

I thought that if these hostels were regarded as alternatives to prison, it had to be remembered that if men broke the law they had to be punished and not excused on mental grounds. I referred to Judge Tumim's recent report on Brixton Prison advocating a substantial improvement in prison medical facilities (see page 123). Did Lady Faithfull think the standard of psychiatric care in prison hospitals should and could be brought up to the level of that provided in psychiatric hospitals?

She did not agree that this could be achieved on a large scale, and thought that special prisons with a psychiatric bias were more practicable. I enquired whether she thought mentally disordered offenders in general could be dealt with in psychiatric prisons like Grendon, or whether they should go to a special hospital like Broadmoor. She admitted she was in a dilemma over this point. She would like prison hospitals to come under the health service and not the prison service. On the other hand, if the places she had in mind were known as prison hospitals, they would be more acceptable to the general public, as embodying the concept of punishment.

Staffing levels would in any case have to be considerably raised. She was attracted by the idea of the Home Office and National Health Service setting up prison hospitals under a joint umbrella. I expressed my sympathy with her, but wondered how far this would work out in practice. Lady Faithfull said prison officers should be attached to a good mental hospital for a year, not only to learn the technique, but to acquire the attitude which can only be acquired in this way.

So, once again, we are left to conclude that a new, far more intimate collaboration between the Home Office and the National Health Service is indispensable if mentally disordered offenders are to be better treated.

Lord Harris of Greenwich

Former Minister of State at the Home Office; Former Chairman of the Parole Board

Lord Harris was at one time personal assistant to Roy Jenkins when Home Secretary, and later became Minister of State at the Home Office, and later again Chairman of the Parole Board. He was thus responsible for the police force for five years and for prisoners for two-and-a-half years. He has had a continuing relationship with the police force as Chairman of the Police Foundation, an independently funded organization. This unusual connection with the police has given him a valuable insight which complements the generally held one where prisoners are concerned.

On 10 June 1988 he opened a debate in the House of Lords on 'Mentally Disturbed Prisoners: Remand' by asking the government what action they proposed to take regarding mentally disordered prisoners being kept increasingly in police cells. In an earlier debate he had quoted as an example the case of Michael Flynn, remanded in police custody despite persistent efforts in the courts to have him sent to a mental hospital under Section 85 of the Mental Health Act 1983. These efforts failed, and shortly afterwards Michael Flynn hanged himself in Brixton Prison. Lord Harris is aware that the more senior police officers appreciate the difficulties of the system. In the present debate he quoted three other examples of mentally disordered prisoners having been grossly maltreated.

In reply to the question as to whether he has any general comments to contribute about the way the prison system has developed, Lord Harris takes one aspect seriously: he believes there is a conspiracy of silence regarding the behaviour of some branches of the Prison Officers' Association, whose influence is greatly damaging to a number of prisoners. He also feels that some penal reform organizations are involved as well, and finds it sad that they have not said anything about it.

Remand prisoners are being far worse treated now than when he was at the Home Office. Police cells in which remand prisoners are being held are unimaginably squalid in some instances. As a result of being held in police custody rather than in prison department establishments, they are denied all privileges to which they are entitled. They do not have the same visiting rights, do not have a member of the board of visitors to come round and talk to them and to be available for them to raise problems with. There is no governor who they can ask to see. It is ludicrous to imagine that a chief constable, with all the other heavy responsibilities he carries, can possibly take the place of the governor of a prison department establishment. There is therefore nobody at all supervising what is going on. 'The police have no skills as jailers,' he said. Quite a number of these prisoners are mentally disturbed and the police have had no training in looking after such cases.

In the debate on mentally disturbed prisoners Lord Harris also stated:

> I do not want to be unfair to the DHSS, but many consider that, for many years, even before the present government's period of office, the department has been shuffling off the responsibilities on to the shoulders of the Home Office. If it is determined to clear out large numbers of mental patients from hospitals into what it is pleased to describe as 'treatment in the community', in the certain knowledge that the resources for such treatment are scandalously inadequate, it should at least be asked to give an assurance that when consultants are asked to examine mentally ill patients in prison department custody, such requests will be given absolute priority.

Lord Harris takes the view that there has been a long-standing refusal by the Department of Health to take this responsibility seriously. He had attended a meeting with the DHSS in 1978 on the subject of secure units in mental hospitals, for which parliamentary sanction was called for. Sums of money had been voted for these secure units, but it was later discovered that the money had been applied elsewhere. Far from being used to create secure units, to which many inmates in prison should have been sent, thus getting them out of the prison system, the money was being used for other NHS purposes. It was the view of the DHSS that this was a matter for the chairmen of regional hospital boards, whereas it was the view of Lord Harris that the misapplication of these resources was objectionable in principle. Later the public accounts department of the House of Commons censured the DHSS for having allowed this to be done.

Another problem which arose when Lord Harris was at the Home Office was the attitude of some psychiatric nurses. When the question arose as to whether they were prepared to take an inmate into hospital who had a tendency to violence, perhaps even to psychopathy, the question was determined by the nurses rather than the consultant psychiatrist. He suspects that this continues to the present day.

I pointed out that Professor Gunn would say this was the sort of excuse the mental hospitals would give, because they were so full at the time. Lord Harris said:

> The present issue about these cases is as to how they are going to be handled under the new parole system, when they will have a period of supervision in the community, presumably under a probation officer, whose enthusiasm for looking after them is not very great. In future, they will have to do it. There will be more supervision under the new plan than at the moment. The probation service is going to have to learn how to deal with these cases in future. It will require serious training for probation officers to be able to cope with these very disturbed people.

I asked him about psychopathy. Psychopathy, explained Lord Harris, is difficult to define and it is difficult to know how to deal with psychopaths. At the time of trial, the person may have not been diagnosed as such. If they had been, they might have received life imprisonment, but that depends on sufficient psychiatric evidence being laid before the trial judge. Often, psychopaths are only diagnosed once they are in prison. Lord Harris does not object to a life sentence for a man who has committed a violent rape, if there is a proper procedure for securing eventual release. Henceforth the process should be judiciarized, that is to say the decision should be made by a judicial tribunal armed with full executive powers. These cases are discretionary life sentences.

As Lord Harris pointed out in the debate in June 1988, on the face of it there has been failure in the penal system, not only on the part of psychiatrists, but also in the courts. He took up a point made by Paul Cavadino of NACRO to the effect that there should be a number of courts in London to which people could be sent if they had problems of a psychiatric nature, and to which a duty psychiatrist would be attached.

Lord Winstanley of Urmston
Spokesman on Health for the Liberal Democrats

I asked Lord Winstanley whether as a doctor there was an approach to criminals as people convicted of crimes which involved the recognition that there was a mental factor to be taken into account. Lord Winstanley said there certainly ought to be, but to what extent there is he was doubtful. There was a time when he visited prisons frequently and used to receive letters from prisoners and their families. The latter were often disturbed because the prisoner was not receiving any attention at all.

I asked him whether he would divide 'mental' prisoners into those who ought to receive treatment and those who should not be in prison at all. Did he consider that much more could be done for those concerned particularly if the prison medical service were to be integrated with the NHS? Lord Winstanley pointed out that one would be dealing with people in different categories. The medical service has always been reluctant to diagnose people as schizophrenic. Once diagnosis has been made, the opinion is held that that person is disadvantaged for life. There are many undiagnosed schizophrenic patients at large in the community – people in hostels and Salvation Army homes are frequently found to be schizophrenic.

Lord Winstanley explained that he is interested in schizophrenia in many ways. In almost all cases the schizophrenic's condition brings him or her into conflict with society and with the law. Those who need treatment need to have it almost continuously, otherwise they break down. It is almost diagnostic of schizophrenia that a patient who has been in hospital and had treatment, then been found sufficiently normal to return to the community, will almost immediately cease his or her treatment and before long break down again. It is absolutely imperative that they resume treatment.

The only circumstance, Lord Winstanley felt, in which schizophrenics should be in prison is if the prison has facilities to give the necessary treatment. Very few prisons have this facility. What happens as a rule is that the prisoner has a breakdown and is then transferred to hospital. At the present time they are being sent to psychiatric hospitals. Prison officers with no training in looking after mentally disordered patients should not be placed in a position to have to look after them.

A more difficult case is the criminal psychopath. There is a lot more understanding of criminal psychopathy, but no treatment available. However, one thing is certain – with the passage of time as they mature, they can all improve. So somehow these people, who are a danger to society, have to be controlled in some way so that society is not menaced until such time as they can be released – though Lord Winstanley emphasized that these are his personal views.

He added that it seems to him absurd that what is alleged to be a comprehensive NHS should not have the PMS incorporated within it. The PMS should be part of the NHS and not totally separate. He himself would welcome any move to integrate the two services. He realized that prison medical officers were often unhappy dissatisfied people, aware that they were not able to do a good job.

Lord Winstanley agreed wholeheartedly that there were many people in prison in different parts of the country who should not be there, and that they were damaging to others in prison and to themselves personally. Take paedophiles, for example. To the best of his knowledge, there is no completely satisfactory form of treatment. He could not accept the view that results were being obtained which gave rise to satisfaction. He did not consider that many paedophiles were able to be restored to normal life – they were always liable to re-offend. The best course available for those for whom no beneficial treatment appeared to exist, if it was thought that they were likely to be a danger to society, is intensive supervision. But that depends on adequate resources being made available. In any case, intensive supervision has to be carefully done by people of the right quality. This does not necessarily involve special training, but calls for people with the sensitivity to influence someone without becoming a permanent 'minder'.

Lord Winstanley reflected that there has been a marked change of attitude, a general move away from institutional treatment. The fact has been overlooked that properly run and properly administered institutions could in fact serve a very useful purpose, but there are not many left. On the other hand, there was no question that smaller units were the best solution, like the new regional secure units.

Although in one sense he had changed his views somewhat, Lord Winstanley was not opposed to the closure of the big medical institutions where the environment was depressing. The need was for secure units with an appropriate environment and where people can be kept confined. Some need to be locked up, but careful thought has to be given to the environment in which this is done.

Small secure units cost money, however. Throughout the NHS there are many small hospitals serving an important function, where elderly people can be nursed under good conditions. Alas, these are being closed or absorbed into the larger places. Lord Winstanley was not aware of any savings as yet available through this policy. As with any organization so large and complex, the NHS, which has been evolving over 40 years, has not evolved to perfection.

I asked him whether, as a doctor, he thought distinctions should be drawn between, for example, the Kray brothers, where one is being treated in Broadmoor and the other punished in prison. Where should the line be drawn? Here, Lord Winstanley replied, a totally different subject was being introduced. One had to look at the whole concept of punishment. What is punishment for? Is it expected to make human beings better than before they were punished? He maintained that if it were being assumed that some kind of effective treatment were available, this was not the case.

V Some Authorities

Lord Donaldson of Kingsbridge
Former Chairman of NACRO; Former Chairman of the Board of Visitors, HM Prison, Grendon

Lord Donaldson was an obvious target for an interview. He has been one of the ministers for Northern Ireland and Minister for the Arts. He was for some years on the council of an approved school near Bristol, and he was the highly effective secretary of the Pakenham Committee on the After-Care of Prisoners. In 1963 he became chairman of the board of visitors of HM Prison, Grendon, which, when he was appointed chairman, had not yet been opened.

Lord Longford:	You were chairman for ten years of the National Association for the Care and Resettlement of Offenders [NACRO].
Lord Donaldson:	That happened as a result of a report I did for you. I met people who were trying to alter the Discharged Prisoners Aid Society and turn it into something better. I formed a group of which I was chairman and which became NACRO.
LL:	I want to ask about the achievements of Grendon and whether they should be extended. You were Chairman of the Board of Visitors there from 1963 to 1969. There are certain features at Grendon which make it unique in Europe.
LD:	It has what is called a psychiatric régime. It has an additional motive beyond containment and reasonable treatment. Each case was treated as a patient. Dr Gray, the first doctor there, was a dynamic psychiatrist. Today they have a non-medical governor who claims, however, that the therapy is still under 'psychiatric leadership'. In the early days one of the things they found was that a lot of the younger men

had tattoos which they said marked them, and they felt they would not be right for them. The specialist doctor spent many hours taking them off, which was of psychiatric benefit. They said they wanted to change their personality, and it was done.

LL: Could this system be applied widely?

LD: There are two things about it which are unknown in most prisons. First of all, only volunteers came there, and secondly, if they did not co-operate they were sent back to the prison they had come from. This was called 'the ghost train'. It did not happen very often, but now and again with people they could not help. Dr Gray took the view that you could not overcome the sort of mental trouble that these chaps had unless they played their part with you. The same principle as that you cannot cure a man of drinking unless he wants to be cured. The attitude of the inmate to the régime as a whole, and to the medical and trained nursing staff there, was different from the attitude elsewhere.

LL: Has this relationship between staff and patients been stuck to ever since?

LD: There have been risks, but governments have seen the point and said they would not cancel it. Selvey, the present governor, is very anxious to preserve it.

LL: It is claimed there is self-government within the prison.

LD: In my time there were three or four wings and there was always a group who met once a week. It was chaired by one of the psychiatrists. They discussed the regime and what ought to be done and made up their rules. If anyone broke the rules, this was firmly pointed out at a group meeting. Self-government is an over-statement, but they made their own local rules.

LL: This was in 1963.

LD: There have been changes at different times, but the principles have not really altered. From the beginning it was clear that Dr Gray was an exceptional man. He had no nonsense with the Home Office and took certain risks. He would take a man with a bad background out with him, if he thought he could trust him, and he never came unstuck. He was prepared to take the risk. One particular man worked in the library – a strong-arm man in a drive-away killing. He became interested in painting and ended up selling pictures – entirely because Gray let him go and look at things.

LL: I accept the view that it has worked.

LD: Quite a number had very severe mental disorders. Schizophrenics were hospital jobs. That was accepted. In my day, by the time I left after five or six years, the results were approximately normal on average, but the longer people stayed, the better they did.

One of the things inmates did, and I am sure is done elsewhere, at their weekly meetings was to state their problems. It is then a great relief to someone who has a problem of a sexual kind to find that other people do too. This is called group therapy, but was done very early on at Grendon. It does not apply to everyone. Gray always said, 'First of all, you must get people who want to come and see you. And when I see them, I decide whether I can do any good. If I can't, I send them back.'

LL: Could these principles be applied more widely? Is there a difference between therapy and training?

LD: They are two quite different things. Training is learning a skill, with the discipline required. Therapy is trying to put right a known functioning evil.

LL: Should there be another Grendon?

LD: I would say yes, there should be one in every major prison district. Statistics would have to be worked out. You could certainly have five Grendons, all doing the same thing, but would have to be careful as to who was in charge. Anybody starting in the PMS should go to Grendon and come away with ideas.

Grendon Underwood was established in 1963, and a word about it is necessary here. Certain underlying principles have been adhered to throughout, though there have been important developments in recent years:

• The régime is therapeutic, not penal. It has even been said that Grendon Prison is a hospital more than a prison, whereas Broadmoor Hospital is a prison more than a hospital.
• The leadership is psychiatric, but the total approach is multidisciplinary. For many years the governor was a doctor, but for some years now he has been an enlightened layman.
• The inmates, as they are called, are carefully selected as men with personality defects, but not 'nutters'.
• The inmates must accept responsibility for their conduct.
• All patients have volunteered to come to Grendon although, of course, they were sent to prison by the courts.
• The treatment is essentially community treatment. The group therapy is one major aspect of this. It is, however, part of a wider process under which the inmates 'treat' themselves. This links up with a wide measure of self-government, as much as is possible in the prison.
• No violence is permitted. The inmates were recently asked whether as a general rule both the aggressor and the victim of violence must be removed from Grendon. They agreed the principle.

At one time 80 percent of the inmates went back to prison, 20 percent into the community. The position is reversed: now 80 percent go into the community and 20 percent to prison.

Penal reformers, including myself, have again and again demanded there should be at least one other Grendon. There is at last a glimmer of hope from the Home Office that this may be so. Why is it, however, that the Home Office have been so reluctant for so long to take such a step? One can only assume they regard Grendon as more expensive than an ordinary prison. They would probably argue that 400 prisoners instead of 250 could be housed in Grendon if the prison were run on normal lines. It is true that the staff ratio is higher, but not, I gather, extravagantly so, except under Thatcherite criteria.

Grendon has been admired by penal reformers at home and abroad for many years, but I gather it has not been imitated. The question that has inevitably been asked is, does it work? Up until now no studies have been able to demonstrate that the rate of recidivism is any lower for prisoners who have gone to Grendon than other prisoners. These figures need not be regarded as final. In any case, I accept the opinion of the medical director that the inmates of Grendon are better people, although I think he likes to refer to them as better-functioning people.

Can the principles of Grendon be extended with profit elsewhere? One must remember that Grendon has the advantage of being able to dismiss those who do not fit in, which is an option not available to the prison system as a whole. Personally I feel there are many prisoners who would benefit from the Grendon régime and who would be ready to accept its rules of conduct. It is difficult, however, to see how a prison system involving punishment in the interests of law and order could be dominated, as in Grendon, by therapeutic and not penal considerations. It remains a notable aspiration.

Judge Stephen Tumim
Her Majesty's Chief Inspector of Prisons

I began by explaining to Judge Tumim that I was concerned with the proper treatment in prison of people with mental disorders, how to get them transferred to hospital and back again, if necessary. Judge Tumim replied that what had happened was rather surprising. It had been expected that with the closing down of the mental hospitals there would be a great many more mentally disordered people in the prison system. This had not so far been the case.

The question was: should we be improving the medical provision in prison hospitals? If we do, is there then the danger that courts will send more people to prison on remand, when they should be making hospital orders and transferring them to mental hospitals? Judge Tumim feels that, whatever happens, we have still got to improve conditions in prison for mentally disordered offenders. The way to do that depends on the kind of prison one is talking about. In his recent report on Brixton Prison he states that 'Consideration should be given to providing within the Hospital a psychiatric intensive-care ward with daytime activities and appropriate staffing so that it can be designated as a hospital within the meaning of Part II of the Mental Health Act 1983.' Brixton Prison has a thousand young people on remand at a time. If you are dealing with a small prison in the country, such a specialist unit is neither cost-effective nor necessary. But in Brixton it is possible and it is needed.

In his other recent report, *Suicides in Prison,* Judge Tumim set out quite beyond suicide a code of practice to reduce the level of anxiety in prison. He deliberately specifies how it is to be done:

3.10: *General conditions:*
It is essential that steps are taken to confirm the dignity of the individual, especially where a person's esteem is most threatened. To help preserve their state of mind, every inmate should have the right to expect some fundamental standards, namely:
(a) a clean bed with tear-proof mattress covers and sufficient space in which to live;
(b) access to a toilet and wash basin at all times with a daily shower;

(c) a reasonable degree of privacy;

(d) clean, presentable and properly fitting clothing;

(e) healthy food and a balanced varied diet;

(f) careful medical attention which should provide standards equivalent to those in the community;

(g) the opportunity to communicate by way of visits, letters and telephone calls; and

(h) the opportunity to receive assistance from staff about personal problems and preparation for release.

. . . We would like to see the development of a list of expectations agreed by the Governor and Area Manager whereby every inmate arriving at a prison is given a paper informing him of the minimum he can expect in terms of service and provision.

These are the things he would like every inmate to have, including careful medical attention. In a big remand centre like Brixton, it is difficult to know the number of people who are mentally disordered. But the number who attempt suicide and who are disturbed is assessed as being one in three. A lot of people have no diagnosable mental illness, but nevertheless attempt suicide. If a man is feeling depressed and is shut up all day in a small, airless, smelly cell with two other uncongenial cell-mates, it is hardly surprising if he tries to cut his wrists.

When turning a prison hospital into something like an NHS hospital, it is not a question of employing a few more psychiatrists, but of greatly increasing the number of trained nurses. Judge Tumim's recommendations are set out in his report: 'There should be a nursing presence in reception when inmates arrive from court.'

The recommendations are not limited to the question of staffing. Judge Tumim would like day centres set up in the big prison hospitals, modelled to some extent on an innovative type known as a 'hanger' in Broadmoor. There patients are persuaded to come out of their rooms and spend the day socializing with others on a wider basis than under ordinary prison association periods. They can wander about, watch television, study painting and modelling with the guidance of a teacher, all under the supervision of a nurse or nurses. In other words, the day centre has the atmosphere of a mental hospital rather than that of an ordinary prison. The centres would not be appropriate for smaller prisons.

The usual argument that will be raised against the idea by the Home Office is, of course, that courts will be encouraged to send to prison people who should be sent to hospital. That is something which would have to be faced. There is some truth in the criticism, but not enough to act as an impediment against trying to improve hospital conditions in Brixton.

It came to Judge Tumim as a revelation as a judge on his first visit to mental hospitals to find so many people convicted of murder who had been in hospital far longer than they would have served in prison. The burden of proof is a most obvious definition. To send someone to prison, you have to be satisfied they are guilty. To let people out of Broadmoor, you have to be satisfied they are safe. If patients are there under a restriction order, the tribunal has to be satisfied that they are indeed safe to be let out. Judge Tumim felt that this was a difficult, a different burden.

With regard to transfer from prison to hospital, for example, or vice versa, the transfer provisions are clearly stated in the Mental Health Act 1983 and Judge Tumim considered them perfectly adequate: Sections 3.45/6 deal with the court remanding people to hospital as against prison; Sections 3.47/8 provide for getting them back again, transfer directions and restriction directions. If somebody is in prison, sentenced to ten years and is mentally ill needing hospital treatment, when he recovers he can be returned to prison.

On the whole, people who need very high security tend to end up in prison rather than hospital. Norfolk House in Broadmoor seems to Judge Tumim to be as secure as any prison. He said he was becoming less convinced that it is necessary to put people in mental hospitals. The whole move has now gone the other way. Psychopaths used to be put mostly into the special hospitals, but now much less so. There is nothing the mental hospitals can do for psychopaths.

One of the difficulties, as Judge Tumim points out in his reports, is the drafting of NHS personnel to run a prison hospital. It would need careful organizing, but he was not at all sure that the Department of Health would agree to it. This is one of the problems – putting an NHS hospital into Brixton Prison. It would have to be a special unit.

The Home Secretary's statement of 14 December 1990 on Judge Tumim's *Suicides in Prison* said that a working party would be set up to consider the matter as to whether they could install an NHS hospital in Brixton Prison. 'I welcome,' states the Home Secretary, 'Judge Tumim's particular focus on the vulnerability of young prisoners. The Government recognizes the need to minimize the use of custody for young people. . . . We are committed to provide a full and relevant programme of work, education, training, physical education and other activities for those serving prison terms.'

Judge Tumim participated in the second half only of the Woolf Report into the prison disturbances in April 1990, the half dealing with recommendations. He had been called upon to give advice and, on the whole, was in agreement with the findings. One of the main causes of the disturbances had been prisoners' grievances, and in particular that nobody listened to their complaints. It was to these matters that Lord Justice Woolf's inquiry had substantially addressed itself.

I enquired whether Judge Tumim would wish to reform the 1983 Mental Health Act? He considered that the passages on transfer were all right. The problem was largely due to the lack of use of them, as well as the lack of clarity. It was much easier for magistrates to remand somebody to Brixton, say, than to call in a doctor. With regard to the requirement as to treatability, doctors interpreted this differently in various parts of the country. He himself preferred to keep the definition loose. Some courts claim that it is too difficult to get an offender into hospital and so send him to prison instead. That is the real problem.

In the report on suicides in prison a comparison is made between psychiatric care in prison and care in the NHS, passages having been prepared by Judge Tumim's psychiatric consultant. He considered them useful. The introduction to this section describes 'in an impressionistic way the differences between care in the two services' and goes on to say this of the mentally disordered:

3.41
'mental disorder' means mental illness, arrested or incomplete development of mind, psychopathic disorder and any other disorder or disability of mind and 'mentally disordered' shall be

construed accordingly. (Section 1(2) Mental Health Act 1983.)

Judge Tumim drew attention to another interesting passage:

3.66
In the case of addicts, prison may be more effective at withdrawing inmates from the substance of abuse than the hospital system.

Passages 3.67–3.78 outline the scheme for psychiatric assessment at court. They deal with some experiments in developing court psychiatric assessment programmes at Bow Street, Marlborough Street, Horseferry Road, and West London, respectively. When an offender appears to be mentally disturbed, a doctor is called in to assess him straight away. This has proved to be a most interesting experiment, but can only work in a busy city where doctors are available. If the doctor decides that the man should not be tried, magistrates will accept his advice and send the man straight to hospital. Judge Tumim was not talking in terms of Broadmoor, but of the ordinary mental hospital, for cases such as compulsive shoplifting, acute depression and so on. Treatment by medication can be effective if the patient abides by it.

I referred to the NHS and enquired whether Judge Tumim was conscious of its inadequacies. He assured me that he was much more conscious of the PMS. He would like to see more of the NHS in prisons. He recommended the book *Prison Health Care*, by Richard Smith, which focuses on dismantling the PMS and replacing it by the NHS. However, Judge Tumim himself does not recommend this solution. A lot of prisons are very different from Brixton and Wormwood Scrubs, where he would like to see prison hospitals run on the lines of a school sanatorium or sick-bay.

The major part of prison hospital work is very dull for doctors, a bizarre form of general practice, excluding as it does women, old people, and children. Most prisoners are healthy young men needing little attention. This is best done in the first place in small country prisons by the ordinary NHS form of part-time working. Full-time prison doctors become stylized. Judge Tumim thought it was necessary to train part-time GPs in how to deal with prisoners, not on the medical side but on the social side. Prisoners tended to ask to see a doctor out of boredom when there was nothing wrong with them. Prisoners can be threatening and abusive to doctors. This aspect calls for special consideration and special training. For the most part, work for doctors in prisons is purely routine, but there should be greater access to psychiatric and psychological nursing facilities.

Judge Tumim agrees with the idea of special units such as those advocated by Dr Bowden (see page 41). But if the PMS is to be retained, it needs to acquire many more of the NHS's administrative skills. A group of doctors do not know much about administration. He would like to see prison medical services grouped much more so that in a particular area it is possible to find all the facilities needed. This of course would need shrewd planning, taking the size of the establishment into consideration. Where there were mental nurses, they must deal with mental cases, for example. There were not a great many people in prison with acute and lasting illnesses. Long-stay people should have their lives made as bearable as possible – a question of management.

If he were a dictator, Judge Tumim would avoid the rigid drawing of lines between prisons and mental hospitals, which he does not consider to be useful. There are a number of people who are better off in prison than in a mental hospital, and vice versa. It varies; a man can adapt from time to time. Grendon is more of a psychologist's haven than a psychiatric hospital. Grendon's problem is that the rate of re-offending by former inmates is no lower than that for an ordinary prison, the reason why the experiment has not so far been extended.

Roger Graef
Author and Film-maker

Roger Graef is the author of *Talking Blues*, a study of the British police, but is best known for his films, most notably *The Police*, a series based on the Thames Valley Constabulary for BBC television. The programme on rape in that series changed the way the police handle rape inquiries.

Lord
Longford:

What are the special problems of the police with regard to the mentally ill?

Roger
Graef:

The problems which the police have in coping with mentally ill suspects are so complex that there is a new code of practice under PACE (the Police and Criminal Evidence Act): They must cease interrogating anyone who they suspect might be mentally ill. They must then find someone in whose presence they can continue the interview: a relative or someone responsible for their case, or any professional in the field of mental illness, or other appropriate adult who is not employed by the police.

LL:

Is it easy in practice to give effect to this requirement?

RG:

No indeed. This last phrase is full of problems – apart from the vagueness of 'appropriate'; such people are few and far between. There is an acute shortage of experts, yet Section 136, Arrest and Committal, calls for a team of three – a social worker, a psychiatrist, and a police surgeon [under the new title Forensic Medical Examiner] – to be summoned and agree that the person should be committed.

Psychiatric social workers are useful but scarce, especially since the cuts. Police surgeons are underpaid and not the most distinguished members of their profession. They are often especially bad at diagnosing mental illness. Many are what Barrie Irving, head of the

129

Police Foundation, calls 'scientistic', meaning that they are stuck with an early twentieth-century view of medicine, only interested in things you can measure – pulses, heartbeat and physical signs. If prisoners are not displaying those signs of stress, most surgeons are unwilling or seemingly incapable of answering questions about their mental state.

Psychiatrists often resist police assessments, especially about dangerous people, when there are no beds in their hospital. They also turn people away because they are from the wrong catchment area. This will increase as cuts and new NHS reforms bite deeper. Too often the police are left with the problem, both for diagnosis and for care and custody.

LL: What about the relationship between the police and the psychiatrists? How do the police react to more complicated cases?

RG: To handle this delicate and complex problem, professionals receive years of training and study. Police have only one-and-a-half hours of practical training (apart from reading assignments) out of some 300 of general training. Moreover, they encounter mental patients often in extremis, or under volatile conditions far removed from the sedate calm of a ward or a psychiatrist's office. They are, it seems from the National Schizophrenia Fellowship's work, astonishingly good at spotting mentally ill people, provided they display the usual symptoms of disturbed behaviour. They are less good in the area of mosaic personality disorders which are frankly hard even for professionals to detect. Many people who are ill seem quite normal most of the time, and can rise to the occasion in a police station.

Many fragile personalities such as obsessives, who manage to live normal lives, more or less by accommodating their obsessions in the normal world, are pushed into extremes by being locked up in a cell for hours. Unable to keep going with their collecting of small items, or walking in long complex patterns, or whatever is their symptom, they become desperate. Many hurt themselves by banging their heads against the wall or door, until they bleed, or they may even hang themselves.

Police cells are totally unsuited for any normal person to feel comfortable in – unlike cells on the Continent which are often simply rooms with locks on them. Even new stations like Streatham and Stoke Newington show no concern for the number of people who damage themselves in cells.

LL: What would you do about improving the situation in the cells?

RG: All police stations should certainly contain safe cells in which surveillance is possible all the time from video or large plexiglass windows. Remember that suspects are still innocent until proved guilty, but the furniture of the cells gives no such impression. Nor does the routine on remand, which bangs people up for far longer than convicted prisoners. It is a recipe to cause mental illness, as well as to exacerbate it.

Of course, prisons too are stuck with mental patients because of the shortage of beds in mental hospitals. Over the next three years, 35 hospitals are to close and 26 prisons to open – a sure indication of what will happen to many of those patients.

LL: You seem to be expressing a deep conviction about the need for a fundamentally new attitude to the mentally disturbed?

RG: Indeed I am.

LL: Although you despise the present state of care in the community, in a sense it does represent your own ideal.

RG: What is the goal of our handling of mentally ill offenders, or the mentally ill themselves? Unless we propose to lock them away forever, it must be their

successful reintegration into society, performing as
safely and productively as possible. That must be the
measure we use to judge all of our steps in dealing with
them from arrest to examination, diagnosis and inter-
rogation, to the custody arrangements and subsequent
treatment.

One of my old friends successfully worked at the
Treasury for many years, during which he spent months
at a time in a mental hospital being treated for manic
depression. It was to his colleagues' and employers'
credit that they supported this régime, and we all – his
family, friends and the civil service – gained from his
productive time. Until and unless we recognize the
degree to which we are all a bit crazy and that the crazy
are also often quite smart, we will fail to create an
environment in which care in the community, and the
successful reintegration of mentally ill offenders back
into normal life, is possible.

LL: Do you feel that you can conclude on a positive note?

RG: I regard the above as positive. My negative views about
prison and the deleterious effects on almost everyone
who passes through the system are based on the test I
suggested earlier: how effective is it in achieving the
reintegration of offenders – mentally ill or not – into the
community? The answer is that it fails completely. We
have no easy alternatives, although some experiments
show hopeful signs of being better than prison. They
desperately need resources and research to sustain their
progress. They operate on a fraction of the cost of
prisons. The common factor of them is the degree to
which they treat offenders with dignity and give them
responsibility and support in being active members of
their own communities. It also helps if we are humble
enough to admit the failure of the current system. It
allows us to be more adventurous in our search for better
answers. We need not waste so much energy defending
the *status quo* by pretending that it is successful.

Roger Graef might accept the description of an iconoclast, but he also helps us. I acquired from him a glimmering of a far better way of treating mentally disordered people and, in particular, mentally disordered offenders.

Dr J. M. Forsythe
Regional Director of Public Health, South-East Thames Regional Health Authority

Dr Forsythe began by saying something that I found intriguing:

> I do find it extraordinary that with the great brains within the legal and medical professions some sort of protocol or algorithm cannot be devised to act as guidance for all the different agencies to follow, to ensure that the individual under consideration is given the appropriate attention. What I have in mind is the sort of procedure that has been developed in relation to child abuse or, more specifically, within medicine concerning the relation between primary and secondary care, for example, for diabetics, asthmatics.

We then got down to questions of practical procedure:

> We both agree that when somebody offends and is arrested, the first step, if there is any doubt, is to establish whether or not illness could be the cause of the individual committing the offence. This, of course, is not always easy as at the time of arrest the individual may not give rise to any doubt, but at this stage I would regard it as being unimportant if the individual is apparently well. If the individual is ill, then a series of questions needs to be answered in a logical way, which will eventually lead to a series of different solutions ranging from secure hospitals to care in the community.

I asked Dr Forsythe to indicate any special areas which in his practical experience are most troublesome.

> There appear to be two difficult areas for which special care needs to be taken:
> 1. The person is not 'ill' but needs some sort of therapy to deal with the deviant behaviour.
> 2. The psychiatrist diagnoses 'not ill, but personality disorder'. It may be that 1 above is a subsection of 2, but I often feel that this label of 'not mad but bad' is one which the NHS uses to wash

its hands of a very difficult area, for which the NHS seems to have nothing to offer at the moment.

Dr Forsythe reacted urbanely to my suggestion that community care is now a farce in the eyes of many well-informed people:

> I feel that the concept of community care is a reality when you have integrated primary care teams incorporating general practitioners, community health staff and social workers with close working relationships with psychiatric nurses seconded from the hospital service.

I questioned Dr Forsythe closely about regional secure units. He told me, to my surprise, that those in his region not only contained patients from a wide variety of sources, 'but they have not all offended'. I do not know whether I should also have been surprised at what he said about the suggestion of Professor Gunn (see page 48) and others, not to mention myself, that the present number of beds should be increased from 600 to the Butler Report (see page 15) target of 2,000. I had better quote his actual words:

> You might be right, but I believe that a number of units have blocked beds through inadequate appropriate facilities, particularly 'asylum' care, and that without the extent of this problem being known, it would not be a good use of public money just to double [*sic*] the supply of one particular type of facility serving a highly specialized purpose.

It is right that the views of the man on the spot should be carefully recorded. I still respectfully adhere to the Butler target.

Professor J. Mahoney, SJ
King's College, London

I wondered whether there was a Christian angle on the whole question of mentally disordered offenders. Were they, when sentenced, to be held morally responsible?

Professor Mahoney observed that he was simply not familiar with the technical side of the matter. What he could offer was some thoughts on the way in which Christianity traditionally has looked upon the whole area of responsibility and the moral imputability of one's actions. One can begin by saying that Christianity is not just interested in people's external behaviour, actions or compliance, but centrally in their interior disposition. What God judges is what goes on in the human heart. How man judges, how society judges, may be totally different.

If the essential is the interior disposition, then what is involved in that? Traditionally there are two areas of reflection in assessing moral responsibility: one is concerned in the knowledge and the other with consent. In fact, if we look at the idea of sin within the whole moral tradition, then we cannot commit a serious sin unless we have full knowledge and consent. Each of these phrases needs to be unpacked.

What counts as full knowledge? If one is looking particularly at those who are mentally defective or mentally disordered, there are three points one could make:

1. There is a difference between what one might call notional knowledge and real knowledge; following Cardinal Newman's distinction between notional assent and real assent to a belief. Take, for example, Cardinal Newman's definition: If one says to a child: 'Do you know it is wrong to steal?' The child may say: 'Yes,' because he has been told this; but it is different if one says: 'Do you realize that it is wrong to steal?' In other words, is this knowledge part of you and not just in your memory?

    You can tell people what is right and what is wrong, but do people take it in, so that it becomes part of themselves? This requires not just a good memory, but the capacity to think and to reflect on what one is told is right or wrong. Knowledge can be superficial.

2. However, it can take time for knowledge to sink in. And this raises the question of how long someone can concentrate for. One's mind cannot wander; the acquisition of 'real' full knowledge takes time. If people are not capable of such concentration, then one can say that their knowledge is impaired – their psychological awareness of it. How long does the child listen and understand what is being told to it?

3. In terms of this idea of full knowledge, the third aspect is to be able to foresee the consequences of one's behaviour or actions. Full knowledge implies not just knowing in the abstract what is wrong, but also realizing what it is going to lead to. An interesting feature of such attention can be that when someone says 'I did not think about the consequences,' a judge may say, 'But you should have.' It is a dilemma in imputing responsibility.

So the question of full knowledge comes down to the level of intelligence of the person concerned and their mental age, or their mental maturity. What would follow from this is that some people suffer from arrested mental development and are incapable of full knowledge of what they are doing. So, correspondingly, their moral responsibility is diminished in varying degrees to the point of exclusion.

Father Mahoney then turned to look at the other point involved in personal moral responsibility – full consent. This opens up the whole question of freedom, he said, of interior freedom on the part of the individual, because full consent means deliberately and freely choosing in the light of full knowledge and awareness. One of the central debates of theology from St Paul and St Augustine onwards concerns our freedom to choose and to act. There have been attempts to show that most of us, if not all of us, are not as free as we may think we are either in general or in particular situations. One theologian has suggested that our freedom of choice is 'situational freedom', and there may therefore be constraints in what we can choose. Someone is theoretically free to give up drug addiction, but there are constraints if they are in a drug culture and have an addiction, so that their freedom of action is correspondingly limited.

All our moral freedom is influenced or conditioned, for instance, by our inheritance, our genetic makeup, our environment and also by our habitual behaviour and tendencies – lying, or being violent – which through repetition become difficult to break. There is in addition a psychological addictive element which Aristotle and others have called 'vices'. So our responsibility can be restricted if our freedom is restricted. And this also brings in the whole dimension of the emotions. With any particular choice facing me, freedom entails the ability to control my emotions, not to disregard them but to control them. Things like impulses and urges can impair my freedom in various degrees and affect blameworthiness.

Father Mahoney developed his theme further: what the Catholic Church has come to realize more in recent years is that the emotions can be very powerful. The Vatican document on sexual morality which came out in the 1970s said that substantially people are not as free as they think they are and this can apply in matters of sexuality more than others. We are not machines when it comes down to sexual behaviour. For example, an adolescent may be obsessed by sexual fantasies and not be in control to the extent that he should be. That is simply a reflection of where he is in his life. Or the person who acts out of fear can be totally mesmerized.

When we talk about the emotions, Thomas Aquinas talks about the passions. He acknowledges their existence in saying that passion can blind a person. As with knowledge, then, there are also various degrees of freedom and consent, and both can be affected, diminished or even negated by what have traditionally been called the 'hindrances to voluntariness'.

Professor Mahoney made a few final points:

• For moral imputability some measure of emotional maturity is required. In a sense one might say that this is one of the profound rules for the whole theme of forgiveness – take, for example, Christ's words from the Cross: 'Father, forgive them, for they know not what they do.' Appeals to people to 'pull yourself together', implying that it is just a matter of willpower, are sometimes totally mistaken, presuming as they do that people are machines and that obstacles can be overcome by sheer effort. That is manifestly not true.

• This is traditional Catholic moral theology but may sound very permissive. It is a pastoral tradition, concerned with the ultimate question for individuals in their choices: whether or not they are in a right relationship with God. God is so loving that he does not let us break off that relationship unless we appreciate fully all that it means, and are fully determined to do it.

I considered that on the whole that depended on our making moral judgments on the conduct of one another. So, if we are wise, we will make those allowances. Professor Mahoney contended that the law has a different agenda and criteria like observance of the law and protection of order and the common good. I replied that 'just deserts' is the sentencing fad of the moment and it assumes that an opinion about culpability can be formed before action. The law judges in terms of other people. Did Professor Mahoney not think that we have to judge each other? Professor Mahoney agreed that there are times when we do have to judge each other. 'But then, I suppose, if we want to take on board "Judge not, lest ye be judged", we have to consider our role in society, so that we can say, "It is the role of judges to judge and the director of public prosecutions to make a judgment on the facts before him."'

I enquired whether condemnation of behaviour was any answer, to which Professor Mahoney replied that the right thing was to condemn the sin and not the sinner. 'If somebody is beating up his wife, I would agree that this man must not be allowed to continue behaving in this manner. But I would not say that this man is a villain. He is doing evil things. But he may not be fully responsible for his actions.'

'Imagine,' I said, 'that a great theologian gives up that profession and becomes a judge and applies these principles from the bench. Is it possible to apply these principles, or are they so far removed from judicial principles that the judge would take great care before imputing blame? Punishment involves blame. The theory is that people are punished in the criminal law system. When you punish a person you are blaming him.'

Professor Mahoney thought some clarification was called for. 'Suppose a mother with a young child smacks him for running wildly across the road – that is punishment, but is there blame on the child's part? Is it punishment or training? It is training.' In popular terms we call it punishment, but perhaps it is not. Some people do not really understand the difference between right and wrong.

'Let us assume,' I continued, 'that we would like to apply these enlightened principles. The question would arise, are we going to say that they represent the Christian theological approach to people who have broken the law? When you get to the mentally ill, would you apply the principles that you have been outlining? When it comes down to training them, you have got to have a Catholic psychiatrist to handle them!'

Professor Mahoney replied that he would not want to apply them straight from the pastoral situation to a court of law. It might be possible to say that a particular serial rapist is not responsible for his actions perhaps, but he would still want to lock him up to safeguard the public and to deter others.

I felt that the attitude of Professor West and some of his fellow psychiatrists towards mental offenders was not really clear. They did not appear to want to say how they should be treated. How far does one blame a pederast? Would you send him off to a mental hospital? Many people would like to take them out of prison and put them in hospital. But most offenders do not want to go into hospital. A life prisoner might prefer Broadmoor, but those with short sentences do not wish to be treated as 'nutters' and remain uncertain of when they are likely to be freed.

'Suppose,' I said to Professor Mahoney, 'you become a judge in the criminal court. Would you seek to apply these principles? They might fit in with your fellow judges, or they might not. It might move you in the direction of leniency.'

'If I were a judge I would administer the law. My understanding is that the whole question of imputability is a very thorny one in jurisprudence and I would want to distinguish between the crime and the criminal. I could envisage someone up before me and I might say: "What you have done is reprehensible. I must prevent you from doing it again, whether you are guilty or not, for the good of society. I must deter other people from this sort of behaviour." I have not said he is morally guilty, but I have to prevent him from doing it again.

'In punishment there is also for some the element of retribution. All my Christian thinking is against retribution. I would want to distinguish between reparation and retribution. If harm has been done, it should be remedied, and I think there is an important element there. But if you take that out of retribution, you seem to say that if harm has been done, then harm must be suffered. I find that logic difficult. There may be a weakness in what I have said. I am not sure personally about this.'

I considered that there was always going to be public insistence on some sort of link between apparent wickedness and the punishment. A judge makes a moral judgment. What about the idea of fairness – the link between the gravity of the offence and the sentence? Most people, the general public, expect something of that sort.

Professor Mahoney was happy with that – making the punishment fit the crime. If one speaks of the punishment fitting the crime, the punishment should fit the behaviour and not necessarily the wrong disposition of the offender. He did not wish to sound categorical, and returned to suggesting that the purposes of the law court were different from those of the confessional. In dealing with crime, one is dealing with behaviour that is socially harmful. The purposes of the law are to try to eliminate it as far as possible. But when it comes down to how one behaves towards the criminal, he could not justify the idea of retribution. Someone, say, has killed a policeman, so he should be punished; that is ritualized vengeance.

Rabbi Albert Friedlander

There is no more profound Jewish theologian at the present time than the Rabbi Albert Friedlander, who I had interviewed for my books on forgiveness and suffering.

When I asked him whether there was any special Jewish contribution to the study of mentally disordered offenders, he began by calling my attention to the Jewish approach to suicide. Originally this was regarded as a grave sin; someone who had committed suicide could not be buried in the ordinary burial ground. But as the centuries have passed, this point of view has now been completely modified, as of course it has in Christianity. I asked him whether the fact that some of the greatest psychiatrists, including Sigmund Freud, the supreme pioneer, were Jewish, had modified Jewish attitudes. He said that that may well be so, but a deeper influence had been the development of the Jewish idea of a loving God.

He has worked much with Christians and is of course aware that Christians are inclined to treat Jesus Christ as introducing the whole concept of a loving God into theology. He says that you can find it gradually emerging in the Old Testament, and recommended me, if I was in any doubt, to turn back to Hosea. He claimed, rather to my surprise, that you can find it indeed in Job, but in Hosea it is more obviously explicit. Turning, by no means for the first time, to Hosea, I hesitated which passage to select, but decided on this one [Hosea XIV v.IV]:

> I will heal their backsliding, I will love them freely: for mine anger is turned away from him.

No one who knows the Jewish people at all well has ever doubted the strength of their conviction about the overwhelming claims of justice, but as preached by Rabbi Friedlander, there is equal attachment to mercy. The approach of the psychiatrists to mentally disordered offenders fell therefore on fruitful soil.

Lord Mancroft of Mancroft

Chairman, the Addiction Recovery Foundation; Trustee, the Drug and Alcohol Foundation

In the debate in the House of Lords on 31 January 1991 Lord Mancroft explained how, for several years, his life had been governed by an overpowering addiction to heroin, cocaine, alcohol and pills. After many attempts to find a cure in this country, he had finally made a full recovery as a result of the experience, professionalism and expertise of the Minnesota Foundation in the United States.

I began by asking him whether he still stood by his assertion in the debate that the treatment of addicts in the United Kingdom is hardly better now than it was in 1981, when it was almost non-existent.

Lord Mancroft:
Very much so. Whereas in the United States there is one bed for treatment for every 2,000 of the population, in the United Kingdom it is estimated that there is only one bed for every 122,000 of the population. Of that number, 90 percent are in the private sector and over three-quarters of them in the South-East. In Scotland there are only 75 beds in all. These figures illustrate the total failure of the NHS to tackle the problem.

Voluntary treatment centres are finding it difficult to cope financially. Most of them do make assisted places available and some take patients on social security. But not all local authorities will pay. The bulk of the funds of the Department of Social Security are directed towards old people's homes. The government appears to consider that the greater burden of in-patient treatment lies with the voluntary sector because it has the highest level of expertise and experience in this field. The estimated expenditure on drug treatment as a whole amounts to £17.5 million a year. It is reckoned at the moment that there are 700,000 alcoholics in the UK and 150,000 people dependent on heroin and cocaine. Between one and one-and-a-half million are moreover dependent on prescription drugs, over half of whom are over 60 years of age. Meanwhile, some £13.5 million is currently being spent in Asia, Africa, the Caribbean and South America on programmes of crop replacement of narcotic drugs.

The cost of drink- and drug-related street crime in London is estimated to be £1.85 million for 1989, the cost to industry (according to the CBI) £3 billion a year. There is a vast amount of conflicting evidence on the nature and size of the problem and complete failure to appreciate its complexity. In magistrates' courts, 50 percent of those facing sentences of up to three years are for drink- and drug-related crimes; 30 percent of hospital admissions are alcohol related. There are 25,000 admissions to NHS psychiatric wards each year for alcohol related problems. Alcoholism is not a psychiatric disease.

Lord Longford:
: Are you encouraged by the government's new policy of drug demand reduction, outlined in the government document *UK Action on Drug Misuse – the Government's Strategy*, which embodies three separate entities – education, treatment and ultimately prevention?

LM:
: I am mildly encouraged. Ministers and civil servants receive their advice from the medical field and historically the medical profession has not been able to help addicts and alcoholics. The other related problem is that the Home Office is responsible for drugs and is unable to influence the Department of Health with regard to funding. The problem has been made worse of late by the splitting up of the Department of Health and the Social Security Department.

Much of the responsibility hitherto for helping drug addicts has fallen on the social services. In reality, addiction is primarily a health problem and should be dealt with by the Department of Health. There are two grounds for encouragement, however. The government's new policy is an important step forward. Previously they have regarded the answer to the drug problem as being one of trying to limit supplies and to blame the 'pushers'. That policy has failed. The reason is that the largest proportion of addicts in Britain are addicted to prescribed drugs and alcohol, neither of which come from abroad.

We live now in the age of the poly-addict, addicted to a whole range of drugs. Most illicit drug users have problems with alcohol and prescription drugs originally supplied as treatment for alcoholism. Patients are admitted to centres inappropriate to treat them and emerge exposed to the same conditions which gave rise to their problem in the first place – the revolving-door syndrome.

The other source of encouragement is government recognition of the funding problems of the voluntary sector by ring-fencing the money to ensure that local and health authorities meet their responsibilities [the National Health Service and Community Care Act]. The voluntary sector is now able to make its own assessment of patients, who no longer have to go from one place to another to get assessed.

LL: If you were a dictator, what would you do?

LM: First and foremost I would start with training. You must train individuals. There is no training for counsellors at the present time. More treatment centres are needed, more day programmes, nurses and out-patienting facilities, voluntary or otherwise.

Many of the people concerned are not unemployed. They still have a job and it is necessary to make sure that they keep their job and their family. We need more half-way houses. It is unrealistic to expect anybody to come out of a treatment centre and make continued progress without support.

LL: What form of treatment is the Minnesota? Is it more controversial – it must be more expensive?

LM: That is a standard sort of jibe. In fact it costs a treatment centre £150 per patient a day. It now costs about £150–160 a day in Britain. Psychiatric beds under the NHS cost £225 per day. NHS beds are no more expensive than those in the private sector, but in the private sector you get infinitely better quality treatment, not in general medical but in specialized areas certainly. An ordinary bed in the Riverside Drug Centre costs from £800 to £1,200 a week. The NHS is financially inefficient; the administration costs are more expensive.

Looking at the price of a bed is only one way of looking at the matter. A recent research study on patients revealed that each – before he came for treatment – had cost the nation on average £190,000 in social benefits, court appearances, hospital admissions, unemployment, crime and so on. The cost of £5,000–10,000 to get a patient 'clean' is a good investment.

Treatment works. For at least 30 percent of patients treatment works, even for the most difficult ones. We do not know that education or even prevention programmes work. The Hazelden Foundation in Minnesota gave me the motivation to become somewhat of an authority on addiction and alcoholism in Britain. The reason the Minnesota treatment is not popular here is that it does not use psychiatry. Secondly, part of the treatment is what is called 'the spiritual programme' which depends on the patient's developed belief in a higher power, on the basis that addicts and alcoholics by the time they get to treatment are spiritually bankrupt. The spiritual side of their life has become completely eroded. To get whole again they have to develop a faith which must have a spiritual basis.

At the start most patients are encouraged to believe that the higher power is the actual group of patients themselves – an obvious and simple way of starting. There are 12 steps in all and towards the end the word 'God' is introduced. The medical profession does not look favourably on that. It is important to realize that it is not religious, but spiritual. I was being treated alongside a Roman Catholic Monsignor, a monk, a Baptist and with Jews from New York, Calvinists and Lutherans. We all mixed, because we had a common desire to get well. There is a choice to channel this aspect into one's own particular religion, but many of the patients are agnostic.

Lord Mancroft does not claim that this is the only way to come off drugs and alcohol, but insists that he has yet to meet anybody who has come off drugs and has regained peace of mind and gone on to become a constructive member of society after using any other method. Narcotics Anonymous is a fine self-help group owing its origins to Alcoholics Anonymous and making considerable headway.

I raised the question of the legal aspect – where did Lord Mancroft stand with regard to the law? Would he change the law? Lord Mancroft said that he believed in the rule of law. If something is against the law, it is a criminal offence. It is a criminal offence to drive under the influence of drugs or alcohol. Most alcoholics and drug addicts only go for treatment after they have reached a crisis in their lives. One of the most useful crisis points of all is a magistrates' court. In America, if you appear before a magistrate charged with driving under the influence of drink, you are given the option of treatment or a sentence.

He is of the opinion that little can be done to stop the traffic in drugs, but we should come down much more heavily on dealers. If the law were relaxed, there would be a massive intake of drugs. There is, however, definitely a case for changing the penalties for those found in possession of drugs – it should be a crime to continue to supply people with drugs. He would not say that possession should be illegal, because it would not work. An enormous number of people do have these drugs. It can be compared with a traffic offence – it is illegal to park on double yellow lines, but it is an offence, not a crime. Possession of drugs should be an offence, but not a crime.

David Turner
Director, Standing Conference on Drug Abuse (SCODA)

'Although there is general agreement that there is some association between [crime and] non-medical opiate use, the nature, extent and significance of the association remains controversial' – so writes Joy Notte, a SCODA senior research officer, in her essay 'The Criminal Histories of Male, Non-Medical Opiate Users in the United Kingdom'.

Some people, for example, believe that young offenders must be delinquent to take to drugs in the first place. Others, however, point out that many offenders do not acquire a record of convictions until after the first difficult age of drug use, 16 years. The whole subject seems to be wide open to every sort of speculative conclusion. No one seriously doubts that drug addiction is likely to undermine the character, and is likely therefore to increase the prospect of delinquency. But the same could be said of alcohol. Yet alcohol is legally permitted and drugs, except on medical prescription, are illegal. Personally, I agree with the distinction drawn and over-whelmingly approved by society. But it would take another book to make out the case and, even then, there would be no coercive proof.

That being so, I felt that my most useful point of contact with the drug scene was SCODA. My special reason for visiting them was the fact that the director for a number of years has been Dave Turner, previously co-ordinator (director) of the New Horizon Youth Centre, which I with others founded in Soho for homeless young people. Mary Tracey, assistant director, has been for many years on the council of New Horizon.

The member organizations of SCODA run to several score. I cannot begin to list them here. A few examples must suffice: Community Drug Project (London); Drug Counselling Service (Northampton); Lifeline Project (Greater Manchester); Phoenix House (South Shields); South-West Regional Drug Training Unit, and many others. Rather to my surprise I learnt that SCODA, with its staff of 13, is financed by the government. In one respect at least they challenge existing policies.

I cannot do justice here to the intellectual assistance and moral support of all the main bodies who are trying to cope with drug abuse. In one respect Dave Turner takes a tough line. He does not argue that those who break the law should be treated with special leniency because they were drug users and therefore not fully responsible. But there is one central feature of SCODA's propaganda and indeed their belief which I do not accept.

The document entitled *SCODA Policies* begins in this way:

Total eradication of recreational drug use is not a practical goal for public policy. The aim of public policy should be the reduction of drug-related harm.

[We believe that] the criminal law should be employed in the control of drugs only in circumstances in which it can clearly be shown to be necessary, justifiable and effective, that punishment should be reasonably proportional to the offence (and that capital punishment is not an appropriate penalty).

We believe that the offence of possession should be removed from statute. To this end, a public review body should be established to detail means whereby there might be an orderly withdrawal of legal provision related to use.

I put it to Dave Turner that these first and third objectives are incompatible. We can all agree that the aim of public policy should be the reduction of drug-related harm. But how is this compatible with the objective 'The offence of possession should be removed from statute'? (This, it should be understood, refers to all drugs including heroin.) Does anyone seriously doubt that the use of drugs, all drugs including heroin, would be much increased if all restrictions were removed? Does anyone seriously doubt that the objective of reducing drug-related harm would be defeated?

Dave Turner and Mary Tracey are far too intelligent not to be aware of this obvious criticism. I am myself aware that the policy of legalizing cannabis has long been advocated by miscellaneous liberals, including the late Baroness Wootton, who headed a government committee on the subject twenty years ago. I was not aware that intelligent people seriously advocated the legalization of heroin, for example. But although Dave did not like the word legalization, that is what the proposals of SCODA amount to. Even so, I do indeed understand how those dedicated to working directly or indirectly among drug abusers would stand much less chance of helping them if they showed a spirit of condemnation.

Dave and Mary drew some consolation from the fact that the police were becoming less ready to prosecute for mere possession of drugs. They and many other dedicated people are trying to break down the hostility of the public to drug users. They felt, for example, that it was most unfair to their cause that Olivia Channon should have been represented as a victim of drugs. Alcohol played a much larger part in her tragic death.

Although I cannot agree with SCODA's declared aim of legalizing the possession of drugs, their work in helping those suffering from drug abuse is beyond praise.

Sally Trench
Founder, Project Spark

In her first book *Bury Me in My Boots* Sally Trench told the story of her life as a teenager with junkies and dossers on the streets of London. In 1970 she set up and ran her own charity, Project Spark, an educational project for difficult and disruptive children, in the course of which 'over six hundred "bovver-booted horrors", unable and unwilling to integrate into society, marched their defiant and lonely way' through her home, a vivid account of which she gives in her recent work *Somebody Else's Children* (1990).

I began my interview with her by explaining that I was preparing a book on mentally disordered offenders.

Lord Longford:	You have had a great deal of experience with disruptive young people. Would you say that among many of these there were some who could be called mentally disordered?
Sally Trench:	I suppose, yes; a small number are.
LL:	Most of this work among disruptive young people: are they the kind who need psychiatric treatment?
ST:	Yes; a small minority.
LL:	In reading your book, I was interested in one particular girl. You say 'My new 15-year-old Spark girl had me really worried. I could smell evil when she entered the room . . . . When the child's mother explained to me that her daughter had tried to kill her younger sister, the child began to laugh – not an embarrassed titter, but with a gleeful, devilish roar. . . . I felt uneasy, for there was a turbulence that was sinister. I felt I had never met anyone so consumed with hate.'
ST:	Yes. That was one desperately in need of help.
LL:	You refer to 'this very disturbed child'. You do not

think of her as a mentally disturbed person?

ST: That young girl had no conscience and I think that is evil.

LL: She was not with you for very long. Did you feel you could help her?

ST: No, I could not, I did not. The last time anybody saw her she was street-walking in Holborn.

LL: At the beginning of the book you say that your methods and your philosophy were different from those of most people: 'Nor am I by nature a do-gooder. I believe I am a person born in complete disagreement with the spirit of the age. . . .' I wondered why you felt that so strongly.

ST: Because I don't belong. I feel that I don't belong. I just feel that I have been born into a world, into an uncaring world, a world that I don't like. I am an outsider. The world needs outsiders like me.

LL: I gather that you have lectured all over the world on your philosophy, your approach. You feel that people are very much interested in them?

ST: I don't feel they are the least bit interested. We live in a very selfish world.

LL: But you do feel you have a special message. Nobody else has tried to do this. You are a very good writer and have an excellent memory for dialogue. You don't take notes? There are some wonderful dialogues.

ST: I keep a diary.

LL: But your approach? I feel your approach is different, because in a sense you have more idealism. To do what you do is difficult to me. You must have a God-given energy to do this.

ST: Everything is God-given. I am completely motivated by my God. I am not sure that he is the same as your God. I am completely motivated because I love my God and he has put me here to help with difficult people.

LL: Has anybody else ever tried to cope with young people like these?

ST: Yes, you did, when you started New Horizon.

LL: Yes, but differently from you and I was not actually living with them. I see a lot of prisoners – difficult ones – but don't actually have to live with them.

ST: I don't know of any other units like this run from home. I have just bought a house outside Oxford, between Oxford and Bicester, Wendlebury. I have raised half a million pounds, free of interest, from loans against this house. When I set my heart on something I just keep going until I get it. I am going to take in ten boys age 16. They have got to be bright. I am going to take them through their A levels and on through university.

LL: Do you think there is a line you can draw between people who are disturbed and others?

ST: I think there is a difference between being mentally disturbed and being disturbed, which is a pattern they have got into. I don't set out to help the mentally disturbed but the disturbed who have gone off the right tracks and need to be put back on to them. In other words, those who have got into the habit of disturbing others.

LL: Do you feel you need any psychiatric help with these people?

ST: I don't want them as bad as that. I want potential 'goodies'. I am talking of boys, probably still in care or living in bed-and-breakfast accommodation, who have been through the children's homes process. They have got to have a certain IQ level. I am taking a very small elite group with potential, and am hoping to draw their potential out of them. I am providing a home with the right environment, so that they can go on and take A levels. I am going to put them back in society and they have got to learn to get on in the world. They will come into an environment which is specially caring. My method is unconditional love, with a good throw-in of strong commonsense and discipline. I am a great believer in discipline.

LL: In the case of young delinquents who are disturbed, do you think your methods are enough or do you need to call in psychiatric help?

ST: My boys were all potential Borstal boys. There were very few who needed psychiatric help, given doses of love, discipline and commonsense. The majority had police records when they came to me; that was why they were sent to me.

LL: You say in your book, in effect, 'I believe I am a person who has been privileged to offer a way of life that gives hope to the young. I can make a speech about that, but I could not bear to be doing it all day.'

ST: Children are children, disruptive or not disruptive.

LL: You call your book *Somebody Else's Children*?

ST: Where is there any definition of 'child'? I see them all as children. At 16 they still need guidance.

LL: Do you distinguish between those who you think can be helped by you and the others?

ST: There is a need for all of us. There is a need for the amateur like myself.

LL: What made Spark come to an end?

ST: When the Inner London Education Authority was wound up. I was told it was policy. That was when I set about writing my book and raising the half million to start off Spark II.

LL: My immediate subject is mentally disordered offenders: there are people who are disordered, but not mentally disordered . . .

ST: It is very easy for young people to go off the rails nowadays and when they do, they find themselves castigated by the rest of society and don't know how to turn round. It becomes a habit. Once they have gone off the rails, they are going to stay off. There is nothing really bad about these young people at all. Given the chance to go back on the rails, they go back. They can get to the point when they don't believe in themselves any more. Once you get them believing in themselves again, they start to improve; they change within days. At last they have found somebody who actually believes in them. I don't think their parents care a damn about them. I was dealing mostly with deprived children whose parents didn't care about them.

LL: In other words they would have become criminals?

ST: Most had police records when they came to me. I had two groups at the same time: the 11-to-13-year-olds downstairs and the 14-to-16s upstairs. I have an ex-Spark boy who wants to get on and get married, and he has offered to come and be one of the workers. At Spark I we had two teachers and myself, but I was not qualified . . .

LL: Only exceptional in dealing with disruptive people.

ST: I am going to choose my ten boys – the bright ones who I think I can motivate, and I think they will all have a history of disturbance. The more they raise their ugly little heads, the brighter they usually are and the louder they shout. All those seeking attention are the brighter ones. Only two out of the 700 who passed through my hands have gone to prison, but every one was a potential Borstal boy.

LL: Looking at it candidly, you can see that your methods worked well.

ST: I would like to think so. My methods were not specific, just very pragmatic, a commonsense way of dealing with young people. My belief in them was my magic. I did sensible things – like stealing their bicycle if they stole from me.

LL: You got into trouble only once?

ST: No, I got into trouble quite a few times, especially with schools. They did not like the way I dealt with the children sometimes.

LL: Coming back to adult prisoners, there are many who are schizophrenic. Ronald Kray has to have regular doses of drugs.

ST: I did not take on any sick persons.

LL: Did Dennis Nilsen have to be a murderer? He had never had any love. Love is very important. There is always lack of love in such cases. You would provide the alternative.

ST: Part of my magic was my own unconditional love towards them, and the environment of a home.

LL: I was surprised at your statement that you feel so much out of keeping with the spirit of the age, because everybody admires you for the work you have done. I don't see why you feel your attitude is resented. I think bureaucracy would be hostile, but not society in general?

ST: Raising money for Spark has been incredibly difficult.

VI Lay Witnesses

Kimberley Andrews

Kimberley is 49 years old. At 16 she was put in a hostel because her mother beat her. She had a stepfather, but never knew her real father. When 18 or 19 she was working at some kennels near Broadmoor while her mother was in a mental hospital. She went to visit her mother there, but she would not speak to her. The mother needed Kimberley's real father, so Kimberley decided to go to Scotland to trace him. She took a small amount of money from the kennels for the journey, this being her first crime.

In Scotland she found out that her mother did not really know who her real father was, there having been too many men in her mother's life. Kimberley stayed on in Scotland and managed to get a job, but was unable to get her insurance cards transferred because of her crime. When she ran out of money, she broke into a shop and took some transistor radios, but was promptly caught. She was held in police cells for two weeks, refusing to give her name. She was then put in prison for 30 days. On being released, she broke the law again and could not face going back to England as a thief. After another 60 days in prison, those investigating her theft from the kennels eventually caught up with her and she was transferred to Holloway in connection with her original offence.

There it was discovered that she could sew and she took up embroidery. This was in the early 1960s and she had never heard of lesbians. When a 'screw' made a pass at her – a sexual assault – she tried to strangle her with a tie and nearly succeeded. The authorities found love letters in her cell and the 'screw' was dismissed. Kimberley was told that if she apologized, she would be let off, but she did not wish to, so she had to do 56 days in solitary confinement. Later she gained a reputation for fighting and would 'sort them out' by hitting them on the nose. She had never been aggressive before prison, but liked the sense of power. However, she did not go looking for violence; she did not consider herself a 'mental case'.

Later she had six convictions for small offences, including drugs. One day when she was free and had found a job in a supermarket, where she became a supervisor, a 'screw' came in and recognized her. The manager sacked her on the spot. Kimberley wanted to go back to Holloway with a knife to 'sort out' the 'screw', so she smashed a window, for which she got a one-year sentence. They found the knife and she was put in solitary confinement again.

In 1966 she was sent to Broadmoor where she spent eight months. She wanted to go back to prison for Christmas because she felt more important inside. 'In there you are somebody, but out there you are nothing.' So she went back to Holloway but was eventually released. She was working at a garage where she obtained benzedrine and dexedrine tablets from lorry drivers, when she was caught again and put inside, this time in Tooting Bec Hospital where she spent two weeks. There she met a heroin addict and took to heroin.

A vicar and his wife befriended her and took her to a Billy Graham rally in Earls Court, where she wanted to go to get drugs. She had wanted to con the vicar and his wife, but came away from the rally conned by them, because she became a Christian. 'I may turn my back on God, but he'll never turn his back on me.' She went to Brighton to commit suicide on drugs and took a lethal cocktail, but came round in police cells, paralysed from the waist down. She found herself back in Holloway where a prisoner stole her tobacco. She attacked her back and was put away in Broadmoor on an indefinite charge, labelled 'aggressive psychopath'. She spent 15 years in Broadmoor and Rampton which was 'hell on earth'.

In 1985 she came out and did voluntary work with the homeless and young people until the introduction of legislation that barred ex-prisoners from working with young people. She was supervisor at the Southend Homeless Centre and got a paid job as a social worker, until the authorities found out about her past.

Kimberley considers that she was wrongfully incarcerated for 15 years. She thinks that the answer is psychotherapy, not group therapy, and that nurses should be better trained. She thinks that mentally disordered women come off worst and should enjoy equal rights – for example, women cannot take a degree course while in Broadmoor. She is emphatic that after-care is essential for those being released back into the community, such care at present a hollow ideal when so many mentally disordered people are virtually turned out to fend for themselves on the streets.

Annette Dunwell

Annette Dunwell, 30, is a young Jamaican woman born in England. When we met, she impressed me with her cheerfulness and bright intelligence.

Annette left school at 16, always rather a loner there. Although her home life was reasonably happy, 'there had been some violence in the family'. She spent some time at Hackney Technical College. When she was 20 her parents emigrated to America. She went with them, but returned after two weeks to live with her sister.

Then came tragedy and horror. In 1983 another young woman threatened her with a bad beating if she, Annette, did not abandon her boyfriend to whom this other girl was attached. Annette, desperately frightened on her own account, stabbed the other girl to death. Then and later she was examined by 'endless' psychiatrists. The verdict, which seemed to her correct, was that she had long suffered from a deep-seated depression. She was convicted of manslaughter and packed off to the then infamous C1 Unit at Holloway. She spent a year there and, as have many others, described the conditions as horrific.

What are more relevant for our purpose are her impressions of Broadmoor to which she was despatched from Holloway and where she spent more than four years. I am not suggesting that they are objective but it seems right in a book of this kind to place them in front of the reader: 'When I heard that I was to be sent to Broadmoor I got the shock of my life. I knew it was no ordinary hospital. Yet I was not prepared for what was to face me.' She tells me that she was already scared at entering the place but considers, even after all these years, that the reception was far more unpleasant than it need have been. After being given a nightdress, 'I was put into a little room with the shutters down. The only thing the nurse said to me was not to try to beat the system.' She had no intention of attempting any such thing.

For three days she 'did not see daylight', except when taken to the bathroom 'to empty my pot'. She has it firmly in her mind, fairly or unfairly, that 'Broadmoor was a prison before it became a hospital' and that this has permanently affected the attitude of the staff.

For treatment she was given group therapy, but for a long time she found it impossible to get involved. It was only towards the end of her four years in Broadmoor that she began to obtain some benefit. In general she argues that 'more independence could be allowed to people'. She feels that patients should be allowed to see their personal files. Personally I can hardly visualize this being feasible. Annette, however, does not despair of Broadmoor. She hopes that her own suggestions are now on the way to acceptance. Nevertheless she still contrasts Broadmoor very unfavourably with Friern Barnet Mental Hospital where she spent two years after leaving Broadmoor. She was moved forward during her time there from strict security to genuine freedom. If only the same had been true of Broadmoor.

Annette is beyond question an honest witness in regard to her own impressions. It is tempting to say that after four years in Broadmoor she had become a much more normal person and presented, therefore, a much easier problem to Friern. It is tempting also to take pleasure in the company of such a seemingly well-balanced young woman and to wonder whether her time in Broadmoor was quite as regrettable as she still thinks it to have been. Such sage comments, however, do not prevent her 'still having nightmares of the place'.

Reginald and Ronald Kray

No book about mentally disordered offenders could omit all reference to the Kray twins, now aged 58, who were convicted of murder in 1969. At present Reggie Kray is in Gartree top security hospital, and Ronnie in Broadmoor special hospital after six years in prison. In past years I have visited them and responded to their undeniable charm and force of personality, without condoning their crimes. What follows is based almost entirely on *Our Story*, their autobiography, published in 1988.

Ronnie Kray suffered from mental trouble early on, as indicated in the following passage from Ronnie's section of the autobiography:

> By November 1956 I was in Wandsworth. I was twenty-three. I was one of London's most-feared gangsters. I had a record and I shot a man. For a poor East-End boy, I had already made a name for myself. . . . But then, with the end of my sentence in sight, my life started to go wrong. I began to go mad again. That's when my paranoia started. I began feeling that people were plotting against me, so I just had to stop them, hurt them, make them see what they were doing was wrong.
>
> Without my drugs, I still get the same feelings today. I was taken to the Psychiatric Wing of Winchester Prison and declared insane.

It was not, however, until 1969, after years of lurid activities, that the law finally caught up with the Krays. 'I sentence you,' said Judge Melford Stevenson, 'to life imprisonment, which I would recommend be not less than 30 years.' It seems extraordinary that with Ronnie's mental background a psychiatric defence was not successfully mounted.

Today, after more than 20 years in prison, Reginald Kray ends with the appeal: 'Look at the wasted years; then come and look at a broken man in Broadmoor and a despairing man at Gartree.' In my view, 20 years in prison should be enough for any prisoner unless the prisoner is declared to be a danger to the public, which I do not believe Reg Kray could be. He should be set free. But it is impossible to say the same of his brother, Ronnie, in the light of the psychiatric opinion quoted at the end of the autobiography.

In June 1987, Dr Tidmarsh (see page 54), a consultant psychiatrist at Broadmoor, concluded:

> Ronald Kray, now aged 53, is a chronic paranoid schizophrenic. In what for him is the unstressful environment of Broadmoor, his illness does not become florid and its symptoms are more or less controlled by medication.
>
> I am sure, however, that he would relapse if he were under stress, as he would be if he were returned to prison. As he is the first to admit, he can no longer stand the pace of prison or, I believe, the competition from other, younger prisoners, and in that environment he would deteriorate rapidly, with the risk of further violence.
>
> In these circumstances, I recommend that he should stay in Broadmoor.

We are told that Ronnie Kray is satisfied with this report and very happy that he will not be returned to prison. Earlier in the book, Ronnie Kray has this to say about his condition, 'I am not criticizing Dr Tidmarsh. He has been very good to me. Sometimes I think that I could not have got through these past few years without him. . . . They say that I am insane. I don't think I am . . . I am all right so long as I have my drugs.' He would be prepared to pay the authorities 'to supply someone to supervise me at home'; he realizes that there is no likelihood of this offer being accepted.

But 'never' is a word never to be used. Let us hope that, long before the end, some unforeseen improvement will occur in Ronald Kray's mental condition.

'Charlie Bronson'

Just after I had sent in the manuscript of *Prisoner or Patient* to the publishers, I received a letter from someone who is now known as 'Charlie Bronson', although that is not his real name. He wrote from Wandsworth Prison to say that he had heard from a friend that I was preparing a book on mental institutions (*sic*) and would be glad to welcome me. He himself has written a book and wondered if I could be of any assistance in getting it published. I was at liberty, he said, to make any use of it and of talks with him in writing my own.

I arranged to see him, having been warned by one of the governors that he was a very violent man. When I called at Wandsworth I was shown into a solicitor's office and the door was closed behind me, not locked. I was confronted by an exceptionally strong-looking man. He told me that he had been a bare-fist heavyweight fighter and now weighed 14 stone. He did 2,000 press-ups a day, he assured me. I told him that I used to do 12 but had long since discontinued the practice. I would see whether I could still manage one. I therefore lay down on the floor and with no little difficulty managed a single press-up. This delighted him. He gripped my hands firmly and said that one press-up from a man of my age was as good as a thousand. So I can be said to have got off on the right foot, or at any rate the right hands.

Charlie, as he asked me to call him, has been in prison almost continuously since he was 21. He is now 40. He was first in trouble when he was aged 14. A few years ago he was at last released but was soon involved in another armed burglary, the cause of his original conviction. He is now doing seven years.

Charlie spent a considerable time in Broadmoor, but they found that he was not treatable so he was returned to prison. He is now being moved round from prison to prison as a result of a recent violent outbreak or outbreaks. I gather that he has been convicted 14 times for violence against staff. I asked him the age-long unanswerable question: why do you do it? He laughed and replied, 'Boredom.' But I am aware that the real answer in his case as in so many others is beyond contemporary analysis. In the last three and a half years he has been moved 32 times within the prison system. I asked him whether he preferred Broadmoor to prison or vice versa.

He said that if he was doing 30 years he would rather be in Broadmoor, but with a sentence of seven years he would rather be in prison because there would be a definite time limit. He says of himself that a leopard cannot change his spots, but must that always be true?

I had written the foregoing before receiving a copy in rough but very readable manuscript of Charlie's book, *Insanity Drove Me Mad*. I will say at once that he has a gift for humorous writing. His life has been so extraordinary, in a painful way so colourful, that it would be a pity if the book were never published. I hope, however, that he will stand back from it and ask whether he was always the victim, as he is inclined to present himself.

At one point, when he was sent to a special hospital, he discusses the question of whether he was rightly labelled 'mad'. 'Prison was no bed of roses. For four and a half years I fought my way through – only to be certified mad.' But he goes on reflectively: 'I never felt mad. I felt tired. Fed up, senses dulled, lack of insight. But I never was mad.' He does not, however, leave it there. 'Or was I? They tell me mad people don't believe they are mad. But I don't see it this way!'

It will be realized that the authorities have never been able to make up their own minds whether Charlie was 'mad', to use his own word. He has been treated or punished in many prisons but also in special hospitals. When I saw him on 18 August 1991 he was in Wandsworth.

From the point of view of the authorities, whatever label given him, Charlie has presented an appalling problem, although the prison officers in Wandsworth seemed to be quite fond of him. This extract from his book describing his arrival at Rampton special hospital illustrates his attitude. He was asked his name and replied 'Bronson'.

He said 'Bronson what?' I said 'Charlie Bronson'. He said 'Call me Sir'. I could see it coming, they were so tensed up it showed in their faces. '. . . – strong expletive deleted,' I said. *'I call no man Sir.'*

He was well and truly beaten up which confirmed his hostility to his custodians whether they were prison officers or, as in Rampton, nurses. In dealing with such a man, whose book is full of human affection towards his fellow prisoners, it seems otiose to go on arguing whether he is mad or bad. Obviously he is an incredibly difficult proposition for those in authority to cope with, but he represents a challenge to a Christian society. One can understand his conviction that his refusal to be beaten by the system is what keeps him going. But someone who could get through to him might persuade him that he could change for the better and yet remain himself.

The dedication of his book is poignant. 'I dedicate this book to my son since he was three foot high. I never left you, son, I was kidnapped and I lost you all.'

Peter Sutcliffe

Sonia Sutcliffe met me at Sudbury Hill station. We walked to her sister's house, had an hour's discussion and walked back to the station. She is small, 5ft 4½in perhaps, elegant without being in any way beautiful and surprisingly unshaken by her recent experiences which have included six days in the witness box in the libel case she recently lost.

Sonia Sutcliffe was born in England. Her parents were, in a sense, refugees from Czechoslovakia, although not Jewish. Her father was at one time in a concentration camp under the National Socialist regime. She was educated in the north of England, eventually qualifying as a teacher. At one point in the course of her education she had a 'breakdown', which she insists was in no way connected with schizophrenia.

She met Peter Sutcliffe, who was a few years older, when she was 15 years old. The last 25 years of her life have been dominated by her connection with this extraordinary man. She was in love with him from the beginning, and was eventually married to him in 1974. Seven years later, he was arrested for his unspeakable crimes. She is far too intelligent not to be aware that everyone is bound to ask how could she not know that he was schizophrenic and involved in such terrible deeds during their married life. She replied in a manner that I found completely convincing. She pointed out that Peter Sutcliffe had worked intimately with countless men in a number of jobs over the years and no one had noticed anything wrong about him.

In due course I visited Peter Sutcliffe and could hardly believe when I met him that he had been the author of such crimes. He is dark, vigorous-looking and attractive in a rough-and-ready way. His story is simple enough. For many years he was haunted (my word, not his) by voices which he was utterly convinced came from God. They told him that it was his duty to murder prostitutes, a mandate which he carried out with horrendous efficiency.

Quite recently, with much help from Jehovah's Witnesses, he has come to realize that the voices came from the devil. He now found it vastly easier to keep them under control. He certainly did not regard himself as a mental case and had refused all medication.

Nevertheless, he preferred Broadmoor for a number of practical reasons, one being the much better opportunity of receiving visitors.

He did not dwell on a point rightly stressed to me by his wife and others. No one can justify the fact that he was sent to prison in the first place instead of to a special hospital. Some time ago I met one of the Crown counsel who advised the prosecution at his trial. He told me that all the psychiatrists alike, for the Crown and the defence, were agreed that his was a clear case of diminished responsibility and that he should go to a special hospital. The judge has been much criticized since for insisting that the case go to the jury, who produced a verdict of murder, so that Peter Sutcliffe was packed off to prison. To quote words used by Sir Winston Churchill, spoken in a very different context, 'Justice, that eternal fugitive from the counsels of conquerors, had moved over to the opposite camp.'

Dennis Nilsen

At the time of writing I have visited Dennis Nilsen several times in Albany top security prison, and have received several letters from him. On my first visit he was in the punishment block, but later he was 'back to normal'. On the last occasion his only request was for facilities to engage in musical composition, on which he has set his heart. On his last letter a friend of mine of many years commented: 'He is obviously an interesting and deeply thoughtful man, seriously trying to explore the roots of his conduct.'

Dennis Nilsen was convicted in 1983 of strangling a number of young homosexuals and keeping the bodies of some of them for some time in his flat. You would never for a moment suspect such a background if you met him. He is tall and well-built after 12 years in the army and a short period in the police. He looks at you candidly through hornrimmed glasses, which he removes as conversation develops. He seems to me, understandably or otherwise, to be sustained by a sense of his own refusal to be crushed by authority, rather like a prisoner-of-war in an enemy camp. From the point of view of the authorities he must seem very difficult to handle.

Possibly he could be approached through his sense of humour. The tabloid press said he had banned a visit from me on the grounds that it added 20 years to a prisoner's sentence. Another specimen of his humour would appeal less to the authorities. A prison officer said to him not unsympathetically, 'You see, Nilsen, where your crimes have brought you. You've lost your freedom.' Nilsen replied, 'At any rate, I have got more freedom than you have.' At that moment, the prison governor came along. We will suppose his surname was Smith. The prison officer clicked his heels and stood rigidly to attention. The prison governor addressed him by name. The prison officer responded 'Yes, Sir.' The prisoner governor nodded to Nilsen as he left but said, 'Morning, Nilsen,' to which Nilsen replied, 'Morning, Smith.' As the prison governor passed on, Nilsen turned to the prison officer and said, 'Which of us has the most freedom?'

Many people hearing about the murders he committed would describe him as mad and be surprised that Nilsen is not in a special hospital such as Broadmoor. He himself, however, is insistent that he is not a mental case and would be horrified at the idea of being transferred to Broadmoor. On no account would he ask for more lenient treatment on mental grounds; he accepts the full responsibility for his crimes.

I have pointed out to Nilsen that at the time of his trial his defence counsel provided a psychiatric case for a verdict of diminished responsibility. He says it was not done in accordance with his wishes. Certainly today he would not wish that defence to be made on his behalf. We have discussed at some length the everlasting question of free will versus determinism. He would see his conduct, like that of other people, as the outcome of his personality as it had developed at a certain time. Certain influences had created the circumstances which made the crime more likely.

He is not enamoured of words like good and evil, but he admits that his crimes were antisocial and 'wrong'. He considers it right and proper that he should serve 25 years in prison as a consequence. He is not asking for any reduction in his sentence, although he would like to enjoy a more fruitful régime in prison.

I put a hypothesis to him: supposing I lived for many more years and, at some future date, gave evidence on his behalf at a tribunal. Supposing the chairman of the tribunal asked me, 'Lord Longford, you have known Dennis Nilsen for many years. If he were released, do you think that he would do the same again?' Nilsen pondered this question for some time and replied, 'It would be most unlikely that the same circumstances which inclined me to the crimes would occur again.'

What, then, of the circumstances that predisposed him to this series of murders? He lays much emphasis on the fact that there was not one single influential factor but a number of them. I should mention here *Killing for Company*, the brilliant book written about him by Brian Masters at the time of the trial. Nilsen is deeply grateful to Masters, who has been almost his only visitor over the years in prison, but says that for the purposes of the book he somewhat embellished the facts.

During his years in prison he has had time to probe his own motivation more deeply. He goes back, not surprisingly, to his early years: 'I was born out of wedlock and a bastard of some man not known to me. It is some considerable psychological burden on a man who doesn't know who he is.' He goes on to mention the coldness towards him in his family: 'There was never any real warmth, affection or physical contact. The developing needs in my life were answered by my creative imagination. . . . The warmth I craved was not available in reality and became the creation of my imagination, in the mirages of warm father substitutes up there in my mind or on the silver screen.' He loved his grandfather but lost him at the age of five: 'The bizarre ritual of his death led to an inordinate fear of death as being the end of love, support and security.' He had many nightmares then about the horror of death.

The next sentence from a letter to me obviously means a lot to Nilsen, though after questioning him I still cannot quite understand its significance: 'In the end my fear of death only became exorcised by ultimately becoming death itself.'

Fear is an element in his life on which he has laid much stress:

The answer why I killed 12 men and injured so many others lies not in the myths of an evil prince of darkness but in the terms of the human frailty. Man never attacks when he feels strong. It is because he feels weak and threatened. In my case I compressed into the subconscious the deprivations of my life because they were too painful to recollect. Pressure built up until it became hard to contain. Ultimately strong drink removed the natural inhibitions and all the lot came rushing out to the act of consciousness.

That, abbreviated, is Nilsen's own analysis of his motivations. I would not think it possible at the moment to carry it further. Thirty-five years ago I published a book called *The Causes of Crime*. Working with experts of various kinds I soon became aware that one should not usually talk of the causes of crime in the sense that crimes are inevitable, but of risk-enhancing factors which make them in some circumstances much more likely. Dennis Nilsen has already gone some way towards identifying the risk-enhancing factors in his case.

The fate of his victims will always be for him a source of unlimited sadness. One must at least give him credit for facing the full responsibility for what he did.

One of his letters expounds his personal philosophy. This cannot be done full justice to here, and I will quote only one sentence: 'Evolution has spewed up a unique being of contradictions struggling to stay in some kind of manageable equilibrium: creativity and destruction, good and evil, strength and weakness, love and hate, birth and death.' He ends in this way: 'Poems are the gossamer of our experience. I wrote this one just prior to this letter:'

Point of Light
FOR FRANK LONGFORD

No Armageddon in its heaven
Riddles of the span
A spectrum in its glory
On the golden sand
Lifting up the drops of hope
Shines the pulse of peace.
Never near but evermore
Rising in the East,
Stirs the light on ribbons pure
Ever after, ever sure.
Redeeming all the soul in rest
A mellow length life will run
Now shining in the glowing West
After the setting sun.

Dennis Nilsen is now involved in full-time education in Albany Prison.

IV
Prisoner or Patient

I   The Prison Medical Service (PMS)

The Prison Medical Service appears to be without friends. It is condemned, or appears to be, by all. The criticism is general and not primarily directed to our own area of interest – mentally disordered offenders – although the latter are thought to be at a particular disadvantage.

In July 1990, a much-publicized letter was written to the Home Secretary by the directors of five highly relevant institutions: the National Schizophrenia Fellowship, the Howard League for Penal Reform, MIND, the Prison Reform Trust, and NACRO. They called attention to 17 proposals in all. One of these has been recommended increasingly in recent times and was particularly emphatic: that immediate steps should be taken towards the integration of the PMS into the NHS.

A document which deserves close attention at the time of writing is the official report on the general medical services, which was published at the end of 1990. It is not known yet what action, if any, the government proposes to take about its findings. Nothing can be starker than this sentence:

> Despite examples of good clinical care, the PMS as a whole is held in low esteem both within the Prison Service and outside, and this affects the quality of recruits attracted to it. The PMS is isolated from colleagues in the wider health care community and is not seen as independent of the discipline role of the Prison Service.

The report shows an awareness, possibly not complete, of the inherent conflict between the medical duty of relieving pain and the fact of prison as an institution of harshness through which pain is inflicted primarily in the interests of the individual and, still more, the community.

Against that background, the report concludes that a closer alignment of the PMS and the NHS would be beneficial, and that the PMS should be managed as part of the Prison Service as a whole:

> Dual accountability of prison medical officers to the prison management and professional lines results in a lack of clear oversight of medical matters, a feeling of isolation within the PMS and other branches of the prison service at all levels. This in turn leads to less involvement for the PMS in wider prison issues than there should be.

It is not my function to pronounce on the administrative changes that would be most effective, except in so far as they relate to mental offenders. Mental offenders are regarded in the report as requiring specialist services:

> In the long term, however, we believe that psychiatric services should be provided wholly on a contracted-in basis. We recommend that once current research into the need for psychiatric service is completed, a full-needs assessment should be carried out at Headquarters and Area level. This should identify means to ensure that mentally disturbed offenders are diverted to hospital as early as possible, where this is indicated. Services should be developed for those who remain in prison and arrangements agreed for prisoners on discharge to be referred to community psychiatric services. These will require close co-operation with the National Health Service.

The report as it stands does not give us positive guidance as to how mentally disordered prisoners should be treated in future. Many, like myself, are focusing our attention on the demand of Judge Tumim in his report on suicides in prison (20 December 1990) that the level of psychiatric treatment in our prisons should be brought up to that in psychiatric hospitals.

I am particularly interested in the question of the training of those who are currently responsible for the care of those in prison hospitals. It is pointed out in the report under discussion that hospital officers undertake a different combination of discipline and care functions. The report considers that their training should be improved, but concludes also that civilian nurses should be used to a greater extent in lower category prisons for particular tasks. Nurses should be brought in from district health authorities.

These issues obviously require much fuller exploration than is attempted in the report. To sum up: the official report on the PMS does not as it stands throw much light on how the treatment of mentally disordered offenders can be improved either in prison or by transfer to hospital. But, as I have reported Professor Bluglass as describing (see page 35), it is a step in the right direction.

For my part, I stand unrepentantly for the complete integration of the PMS into the NHS. Apart from all the other advantages, in that way, and in that way only, will the ideal expressed by many be realized, and the standard of psychiatric care in prisons be brought up to the level of that provided in mental hospitals.

II Personality Disorders

The Mental Health Act category of 'psychopath' is an administrative label more than a medical diagnosis. Personality disorders of varying degrees of severity, which affect ability to conform to social requirements or sustain personal relationships, are very prevalent in the prison population. In many cases these disorders underlie patterns of offending behaviour, such as impulsive violence, alcohol or drug abuse, and deviant sexual acts. The borderline between normal and pathological is ill-defined, and some consider that personality disorders are not illnesses. In a minority of cases, however, the associated behavioural disturbance, which may be accompanied by detectable neurological malfunctions, is so extreme and so far beyond normal means of restraint that a diagnosis of mental disorder, psychopathic in type within the meaning of the Mental Health Act, is certainly legitimate.

In recent years, the number of offenders with personality disorders diverted into the health care system has significantly decreased. The wording of the Mental Health Act 1983 is partly responsible. Section S.1(3) specifies that sexual deviancy and drug dependency are not sufficient in themselves to constitute mental disorder warranting compulsory detention in hospital. Section S.3(2)(b) specifies that psychopathic disorder qualifies only if hospital treatment will 'alleviate or prevent a deterioration'. The first limitation need not exclude those whose sexual or drug habits are subsidiary to more general disturbances of behaviour that may include serious violence. The second limitation, however, lends itself to highly restrictive interpretation.

Current psychiatric opinion tends to regard personality disorders as untreatable, at least within presently available facilities, and by means of accepted medical methods. Even before the Act of 1983, hospital orders on grounds of 'psychopathy', which were never numerous, had declined sharply in the late 1960s and 1970s, coincident with the abolition of locked wards in NHS hospitals, and the decline in the numbers of staff and places suitable for difficult-to-manage patients. As a consequence, some individuals, whose manifest abnormalities, particularly in relation to sex, lead to offending of a kind that arouses great public concern, are committed to prison on fixed sentences where they are unlikely to receive the skilled attention, treatment or training that might reduce the likelihood of their re-offending on release.

The prevailing mood of therapeutic pessimism is not universal and, to a significant extent, it reflects lack of suitable facilities for the assessment and treatment of serious sex offenders, rather than an absence of behaviour modification and other treatment techniques. In the United States, systems for the treatment of recidivist sex offenders have been in operation and claiming success for some years. The State of Washington, for example, commits them under a 'sexual psychopath' law for hospital assessment, and if found suitable, for subsequent hospital-based treatment in lieu of imprisonment. Their subsequent graded release into the community under supervision is governed by judicial review. Of course, the success of any such system depends on the availability of active and specialized treatment units. The use of sexual psychopath laws in some States fell into disrepute when it led to offenders being detained for very long periods without any determined treatment effort.

These issues are of great practical importance in relation to potentially treatable sex offenders. As the Prison Reform Trust has recently pointed out, the Prison Service has difficulty in dealing with them appropriately. In the face of other prisoners' intolerance, authorities have felt obliged to segregate many under Rule 43 (solitary confinement). Attempts at therapy in prison are hampered by this and other circumstances, including the men's fear of being identified as 'nonces', by the constraints of fixed-term sentences served in an artificial environment, and the difficulty in arranging for the continuance of realistic treatment and supervision on release.

The Probation Service now runs a number of schemes for the treatment of sex offenders in the community (to be reviewed in a forthcoming report from the Probation Inspectorate). Centres at

Newham, Great Ormond Street Hospital and the Gracewell Clinic have well-developed programmes, specializing in offenders against children. Their remit does not extend to the generality of sex offenders, but the establishment of these projects contradicts the notion of 'untreatability', and has a bearing on the numbers who might be considered for hospitalization under the Mental Health Act.

It might be argued that any man with a personality disorder, coupled with sexual abnormality, who is sufficiently dangerous to warrant prolonged custody, is a suitable candidate for hospital assessment, provided always that the hospitals (and especially the special hospitals) develop the necessary facilities. In urging improvements to the assessment of offenders on remand, and greater use of Section S.35, the sex offender category should not be excluded.

PSYCHOPATHY

In the comprehensive *Principles and Practice of Forensic Psychiatry*, edited by Robert Bluglass and Paul Bowden (1990), the essay on the psychopathic (sociopathic) personality is by Sir Martin Roth, Professor Emeritus of Psychiatry, University of Cambridge. Sir Martin informs us that in English psychiatry psychopathy came to be conceived as being an ingrained abnormality of behaviour and adaptation first manifest in adolescence and expressed in distinctive forms of aggressive and antisocial conduct throughout life. 'The assumption,' he writes, 'that such a category of disorder was sufficiently distinctive and specific to permit a reliable diagnosis was reflected in the Mental Health Act 1959.' Professor Gunn has told me, however, that psychopathy 'was not a medical term, though incorporated in legislation'.

Sir Martin Roth admits that scepticism has been widely expressed about the use of the word. Nevertheless, he concludes that it is of practical value. In particular, it is of assistance in identifying these disorders of behaviour at an early date and attempting to treat them forthwith. He admits that the treatments so far discovered achieve a relatively low rate of success, but concludes, 'this does not justify abrogating responsibility for the care of psychopathic individuals and the conduct of enquiries can deepen understanding of the influences that have shaped them.'

Someone coming fresh to the subject and reading Professor Roth's essay might be inclined to ask whether a psychopath of the kind he deals with is not what other people would call 'a very bad man'. The full definition in the Mental Health Act 1959 runs as follows:

Psychopathic disorder means a persistent disorder or disability of mind (whether or not including sub-normality of intelligence) which results in abnormally aggressive or seriously irresponsible conduct on the part of the patient, and requires or is susceptible to medical treatment.

Hitler and Saddam Hussein would presumably qualify as abnormally aggressive, possibly as seriously irresponsible. It could be argued that each of them required medical treatment. It would be much more doubtful whether either was susceptible to it.

Sir Martin's essay clarifies the whole subject for me up to a point, though it raises further questions arising from what Professor Gunn told me. Like Sir Martin Roth, he felt that the concept of mad or bad was of value, but later he explained his views at greater length in writing:

I don't think that the either/or dichotomy is appropriate. We all use moral language and concepts in our everyday life . . . Psychiatrists, on the other hand, have technical language which is disconnected from moral language and is morally neutral . . . The health perspective and the moral perspective are simply different ways of construing the universe, and it is perfectly possible to switch the language from one to another.

The Professor's analysis, I suppose, fits in with the definition of psychopathy in the Mental Health Act, which says that the disability resulting in antisocial conduct 'requires or is susceptible to medical treatment'. This is presumably the point of view of any doctor who, confronted with a patient who is clearly unwell (with cirrhosis, for example), is simply concerned with the best form of treatment, and is completely nonjudgmental about his conduct.

One is bound to ask at this stage whether a law court is supposed, in any case before it, to adopt a purely medical point of view. Even where a prison sentence is justly imposed, for example in the case of many sex offenders, it may well be that the medical factor should play a large part in affecting the offender's treatment in prison. But, generally speaking, as long as convicted persons are being punished, in prison or otherwise, it is inevitable that moral considerations, the element of blame or guilt, for example, should be taken into account. If this is correctly reasoned, many who are diagnosed as psychopathic will continue to be punished in prison, though with careful attention being paid to their psychopathic disability.

On the other hand, it seems to be accepted that when the mental illness or psychopathy pass a certain point, the person before the court should be transferred out of the criminal justice system into the health system where there is no praise or blame, and where the best treatment is the prime consideration. I say 'the prime consideration' because, for example, in special hospitals the treatment of the patient is not the only consideration. The protection of the public is also involved. In the classic delineation of the four elements in a just sentence (as enunciated, for example, in my book *The Idea of Punishment*) there are retribution, deterrence, prevention, and reform. Of these only the last two would presumably apply to arrested persons dealt with in the health system.

How does all this bear on the pressing issue of transferring a considerable number of prisoners from the criminal justice to the health system? It is impossible to say whether clearer thinking on the plane of theory would have led to the transfer of Ian Brady or Ronnie Kray, for instance, many years earlier from prison to special hospitals. I would like to think that great forensic psychiatrists like Professor Gunn, when called on to advise in such matters, do not restrict themselves to a purely medical role, but feel a further responsibility as citizens to say what is best in all the circumstances for the community, including the defendant. After all, the psychiatrist must be regarded as something of an expert on the mind and motivation of the defendant. It may be, however, that Professor Gunn would regard this as a betrayal of professional standards.

Such a broader view of the psychiatrist's function is not without risks, however. On the one hand, the psychiatrist would not be inhibited from recommending transfer to hospital by the fact that no effective treatment seemed likely to be available. On the other hand, by agreeing to offer an opinion regarding the responsibility of the prisoner, he or she would be involved in the 'just deserts' process; in retributive calculations which might not benefit the prisoner.

OTHER DISORDERS

Apart from the article on psychopathic personality by Sir Martin Roth, there are five essays in Bluglass and Bowden's *Principles and Practice of Forensic Psychiatry* under the heading 'Personality Disorders'. It seems right to attend to them. They are summarized below:

'Borderline Personality': We are told at once that the concept of borderline personality is a controversial one. It has its historical roots in both psychiatry and psychoanalysis, and in both spheres reservations are expressed as to its usefulness as a diagnostic entity. However, Murray Jackson and Alex Tarnopolsky, the authors of the essay, consider that it is useful. They admit, nevertheless, that the use of the term 'borderline' generates much confusion. In medicine, it is commonly used to mean atypical or even unclassifiable: 'In psychiatry and psychoanalysis it has acquired further meanings dealing with three essentially different concepts which can easily be confused.'

The authors tell us that the term has been used in a descriptive sense to name disorders on the borders of schizophrenia, but among psychoanalysts the term has been commonly applied to certain apparently neurotic patients who are likely to become extremely disturbed, or even transiently psychotic, during the course of psychoanalytic treatment. Additionally it can be used in a way to combine both these definitions. The authors conclude that long-term psychoanalytically-orientated psychotherapy, aimed at intrapsychic change through insight with subsequent modification of behaviour, offers the greatest hope to carefully selected borderline patients.

Again, the authors admit that much may be achieved with more modest aims. They add that 'an institutional framework may be an essential requirement, allowing limits to be set on acting-out and for hospitalization to be available if required during crises'. In other words, whether or not a crime has been committed, it may be necessary for the borderline personality to be treated in, for example, Broadmoor.

A more comprehensive discussion is provided by Dr Ronald Blackburn under the heading 'The Psychology of Personality Disorders'. He casts the net wide: 'Several surveys make it clear that between a third and a half of the psychiatric population is likely to meet the current criteria of a personality disorder, and within antisocial and asocial populations the proportion is substantially higher.' Dr Blackburn is the Chief Psychologist at the Park Lane Hospital, Liverpool (now Ashworth). He presents what he calls a psychological perspective on conceptual and methodological issues raised in the identification of personality disorders. He examines what he calls 'psychological approaches to their treatment'. At this stage I pause and ask myself how the psychological approach would differ from the psychiatric?

Dr Blackburn lays much stress on traits of character. They constitute personality disorder when 'they are inflexible and maladaptive, and cause impaired social function or subjective distress'. Personality disorder, he tells us, in forensic populations is associated most commonly with antisocial behaviour. The overall treatment goal is to minimize further socially deviant behaviour by changing the variables, that is to say, personal deviance. He adds the thought-provoking comment: 'It should be noted that the medical analogy of cure is inappropriate in this context, and the provision of self-control and coping skills is commonly the most realistic.'

Dr Blackburn leaves it a somewhat open question as to whether much has as yet been achieved in this area. He warns us that, while the therapeutic community is commonly advocated as a preferred treatment for personality disorder, lack of follow-up support (after-care) may also partly account for the failure of this approach to reduce recidivism. He quotes Professor Gunn as arguing that recidivism rates are an inappropriate means of judging the success of an institution-based programme, which leaves me asking in relation to the inmates of Grendon or, on a smaller scale, C Wing at Parkhurst, what are the prospective functions for the psychiatrist and the psychologist in regard to these patients?

Dr Blackburn issues a further warning against confusing the terms 'psychopathic' and 'personality disorder'. He seems to regard the latter as including the former, but to be a wider concept.

'Inadequate Personality' is the title of the essay by Dr Patch, a Consultant Psychiatrist at St Charles Hospital. He leaves us with a fairly bleak impression which perhaps is inevitable: 'Although required in a crisis, or to meet a short-term need, admission to hospital does not serve a long-term purpose except to provide asylum, a role that hospitals increasingly decline.' (Would the hospitals argue that they are denied by public policy the required facilities?) Patch considers, 'It is often more appropriate to arrange institutional care in a hostel, coupled with day care in an occupational centre or sheltered workshop, and continued supervision by a social worker or the Probation Service.' But how much of this is provided in practice?

Dr Patch contributes a further essay entitled 'Homelessness and Vagrancy'. He concludes that most efforts at rehabilitation are based on assumptions that have failed. Part of this failure is attributed to the large size of hostels or lodging houses. He mentions with approval small hostels in which men could be helped to relate to each other by acceptance into a 'cohesive environment'. He quotes, however, another authority who makes the opposite case: 'Men rarely stay long enough for the hostel to become a home.' He argues that this 'recalcitrant population should be afforded an opportunity to climb the social ladder', but leaves us in doubt as to whether he thinks it is likely to be feasible, even given much better co-ordination of the services than exists now.

Derek Perkins, Chief Psychologist at Broadmoor, deals with 'Behavioural Psychotherapy for Conduct Disorders'. He mentions the essential components of behavioural psychotherapy under three headings:

1. a precise specification, agreed between therapist and client, of the problem behaviours to be reduced or eliminated, and the desired behaviours to be strengthened or established;
2. the establishment, again in collaboration with the client, of a 'behavioural analysis' of these problems and desired behaviours; this involves setting out the antecedents of the client's 'problem' (and 'desired') behaviour, determined from interview information or other data, and the consequences (both rewards and punishments) of this behaviour;

3. a recognition that factors that resulted in the acquisition of disordered behaviour (historical perspective) may be different from the factors which currently maintain this behaviour (contemporary perspective).

The behavioural treatment of childhood conduct disorder tends to focus on working with the whole family. The treatment of juvenile, and particularly adult, offenders more often tends to focus on the offender. It encompasses treatment carried out both between institutions and in the offender's natural environment. Derek Perkins stresses the need for 'a carry over into the natural environment of any positive changes brought about in the offender's behaviour within the community'. He asks, 'What are the therapeutic skills in attempting to overcome potential barriers to treatment?' These fall under two headings: 'The Structure of the Behavioural Analysis' and 'The Context of the Behavioural Therapy'. What he has to say on the structure is useful if convoluted: 'Within the behavioural analysis can lie clues as to where treatment might most usefully be directed. There can be "core influences" running through the analysis, sets of interrelated antecedents and consequences of the offending (vicious circles) into which therapy can sometimes inject a powerful influence.'

Dr Perkins insists that 'the context of behavioural therapy tends to be as important as the therapy itself. The key issue is that client denial, motivation to change and co-operation in the process of treatment are themselves aspects of client functioning which are just as amenable to behavioural analysis and modification, as the presenting problems of conduct disorder or delinquency.' This may seem fairly obvious, but Dr Perkins says that it is often overlooked. Among the guidelines for facilitating change that he recommends, one is also fairly obvious: 'Helping the offender to understand why he offends.' Obvious perhaps, but easier said than done. However, perhaps the most interesting of the principles advocated by Derek Perkins are these:

Make sure that the unco-operative client attributes as many good therapeutic ideas as possible to himself, rather than to the therapist. The therapist can facilitate this by making reference to, for example, 'your good idea from last week's session', even if it was not quite all the client's own idea.

Capitalize on the principle of 'cognitive dissonance' (Festinger, 1957) by encouraging the client to believe that he is undertaking treatment with the minimum of external pressure; in this way genuine attitude change at the end of treatment is likely to be maximised.

But the Prime Minister might tell us that we do not need academic qualifications to arrive at such conclusions. Intelligence and common sense would teach them anyway.

I have a talented friend, aged 45, whom I have known for about 15 years. He has been in prison many times, never for an offence of violence, always for some kind of stealing. Between the ages of 18 and 20, I gather, he was in and out of a mental hospital and he has been in such a hospital since. He can therefore be regarded as highly relevant to the present book.

He has proved himself capable of helping me considerably with my social work when he has been out of prison. At times he has acted completely out of character in letting me down. But in the many hours I have spent with him, he has never shown any signs of abnormality and has been an entertaining companion. He undoubtedly has an undeveloped gift for writing. I understand that he has been described by forensic psychiatrists as suffering from a personality disorder.

He has shown himself anxious to explore with me this concept of personality disorder. He has raised some very pertinent questions: How is personality disorder to be defined? Are the symptoms supposed to show themselves in conduct or to emerge from conversation, or from physical examination? What treatment is available? How far is it likely to be successful?

Questions of this kind arise irrespective of whether the individual suffering from personality disorder has committed a criminal offence. When he or she has broken the law, the court has to consider what bearing the diagnosis of personality disorder should have on the sentence. Should it lead to a special form of treatment in prison, for example for paedophiles, or should it involve transfer to some form of hospital? In this connection one is bound to ask whether the often strict provisions of the Mental Health Act of 1983 should not be amended or interpreted more liberally. As long as moral judgments are inevitably involved in passing sentence, the problem of so-called personality disorders will remain intractable, as will the different problem of how treatment can best be provided.

PSYCHOANALYSIS

One may reasonably be asked whether psychoanalysis has anything useful to say about the treatment of mentally disordered offenders. Obviously an enthusiast for psychoanalysis will believe that they would benefit from psychoanalysis. The obvious objection is that psychoanalysis requires a prolonged period of treatment and a high measure of co-operation from the patient. These conditions are not likely to be satisfied very often among mentally disordered offenders. It is impossible, however, to ignore the contribution of psychoanalysis to the discussion of crime, even though the contribution in question is directed usually to criminals in general, rather than to mentally disordered offenders.

Paul Klein contributes a valuable article called 'Psycho-analysis and Crime' to the Home Office publication *Applying Psychology to Imprisonment* (1987). Klein tells us that 'modern, more sociologically orientated criminologists see crimes as a form of mental deviance, defined as rule-making'. He makes the arresting statement, 'There is nothing per se criminal about crime. All is a matter of rules, who makes them and what they are. What has to be explained therefore is not crime but rule-making.'

Klein deals carefully with psychopaths in psychoanalytical language. The psychopath suffers from a weak super-ego. This means that individuals feel little or no guilt. This is clearly an advantage in committing numerous offences, especially those involving personal suffering.

'There are other factors, however, involved in criminality. In psychoanalytical terms, the over-controlled aggressive offender has a disturbed super-ego, one that is too strong. This makes for a strong, even cruel, super-ego. Every transgression is to be severely punished; feelings of guilt are powerful.' Klein adds the surprising comment: 'This is the road to the monastery.' He adds another comment which, for me at least, is a sufficient reason for not regarding psychoanalysis as helpful in dealing with mentally disordered offenders: 'An aspect of psychoanalytic theory which is sometimes not fully appreciated is its emphasis on complete psychic determinism, of which *The Psychopathology of Everyday Life* (Freud, 1901) is an outstanding example.'

As mentioned above, psychoanalysis seems to have little to contribute in practice to the treatment of criminals, mentally disordered or otherwise. Klein himself concludes: 'Given that educative procedures in general, and psychoanalytic therapies in particular, have not been shown to be effective, the implications for custodial treatment of the kind that any but the richest society could afford are gloomy.'

Klein finds the ultimate causes of crime in family life: 'Prevention seems the only hope of improving the position.' He demands more research, but the case he presents for it will not convince many who are already psychoanalytic enthusiasts.

III Suicide

A book on mentally disordered offenders can hardly avoid the question of suicide, in particular suicide by those in custody. In the *Report of a Review by Her Majesty's Chief Inspector of Prisons for England and Wales* (December 1990), Judge Stephen Tumim begins by calling attention to the steady increase in the number of inmates taking their own lives. More recently, the figure has increased from 29 suicides during custody in 1985 to 42 in the first ten months of 1990.

Most self-inflicted deaths take place among the remand population. There is a low incidence rate among the female and training prison population. It is not clear from the figures supplied in the report whether suicide in prison is higher than in the general population. In 1988 a total of 5,000 people killed themselves in the United Kingdom. In the same year, there were 30 suicides in a daily prison population of some 49,000, with an annual through-flow of 300,000.

On the one hand, prisoners are much more controlled and in that sense safeguarded in prison. On the other hand, extreme depression is much more likely in custody. It must be remembered, however, that according to an analysis issued by NACRO of prison suicides between 1972 and 1987, mental disorder was among the reasons for suicide in only 22 percent of the cases. It should be mentioned that only 33 percent of inmates committing suicide had a previous history of psychiatric contact, while some 25 percent had previous inpatient admissions. On the face of it, the link between mental disorder and suicide in prisons is not very strong. It is of course open to anyone to argue that all, or at any rate a large proportion, of those who commit suicide are mentally disordered, whether they have been identified as such or not.

The conclusions of the report are notable for the breadth of the perspective. Judge Tumim argues convincingly that the whole environment of prison is usually at its worst and it is seldom at its best – a highly relevant factor when we ask ourselves why suicides occur in prison:

> It should be remembered that confinement in prison may emphasize not only lack of occupation, but also a lack of purpose in day-to-day living. It can equally emphasize the extremes of human feelings in the form of acute periods of hope and despair, leading to frustration and cynicism. Violence towards others or towards oneself should perhaps not be considered as surprising in such an environment. Efforts should be directed as much to the improvement of the general quality of life within prison as to the needs of individual prisoners who may display suicidal tendencies.

Where Judge Tumim does break new ground in a most interesting way is in his carefully argued demand that psychiatric standards in prison, that is to say the care of mentally disordered prisoners, should be much improved:

> Nevertheless, given the facilities at present available within the National Health Service and the penal system, it seems absolutely inevitable from our observations at Brixton and elsewhere that the Service will find itself looking after very disturbed, non-consenting patients for varying periods of time (for example, while waiting for a place in the National Health Service) without any clear basis for treating them. Until such time as the National Health Service is able to respond adequately, the Service must provide appropriate and proper care to these people in prison. It would be of considerable assistance if the prison hospital, wholly or in part (including part for an intensive care ward with day-time activities) could be upgraded and staffed to a standard, so that it could be designated a psychiatric hospital within the meaning of the Mental Health Act.

Judge Tumim has obviously given much thought to this proposal, which deserves the fullest consideration. In an appendix to his report, he sets out a detailed comparison between 'differences for patients between National Health Service and prison hospitals'. From the patient's point of view, there is a large balance of advantage in being an inmate of the former.

On the day the report was published, I raised a few questions in the House of Lords:

> ... leaving aside the doctors, the forensic psychiatrists and persons of that order, what about the nurses? ... How far does the training of prison staff in a prison hospital compare with the training of nurses in a psychiatric hospital? On the face of it there is no comparison. The ordinary prison officer, with a little psychiatric training, does not compare with a fully qualified nurse ... If we are to make sense of that concept [raising the standard of prison hospitals to the level of psychiatric hospitals], how can we make sure that the prison officers concerned receive the same training as they would receive in a psychiatric hospital? In other words, how can the standard of the 'nurses' in the prison hospital be brought up to the level of that in the psychiatric hospitals?

The minister replying did not deal with the problem as a whole, but informed the House that 'prison hospital officers receive six months' basic training, but the prison service is seeking to increase the opportunities for staff to take additional English Nursing Board courses, and is aiming to recruit extra qualified civilian nurses ... National Health Service registered psychiatric nurses receive three years' training.'

I should add that in the conclusions to his report, Judge Tumim also referred to what I have already pointed out: 'Up to 20 percent of hospital officer posts should be phased out in favour of nurses trained to national standards.' For the moment, I leave the matter there.

IV   Panorama

One of the main issues under discussion in this book was highlighted by an absorbing programme by Polly Toynbee on BBC television on 1 July 1991. One or two extracts from her commentary concentrate attention:

> Britain is closing mental asylums, but community care has yet to fill the gap. Now the mentally ill are turning in desperation to hospital casualty departments and ending up on the streets and in prison. Tonight *Panorama* asks: 'Do we care for the mentally ill?'

A little later she goes on:

> The crisis in psychiatric hospital beds is growing because the old asylums like this one in South London are being pulled down. The plan, which had almost universal support, was for community care to replace these old institutions. It was originally a humane idea, but it was eagerly seized on by successive governments as an excuse to demolish these old asylums that cost so much to run, and there were never any firm promises about the level of care in the community that would replace them.
>
> A hundred thousand beds in old hospitals have been closed, ninety more asylums are due for demolition in the next ten years. Tooting Bec once housed 2,000, now it is halfway through closure. Keeping the last 200 people here costs two million pounds a year and the property is valuable. Now it has been left to rot for years, awaiting demolition. In the past, there were long-stay and short-stay people in these hospitals. Grim, malodorous and institutional, few would want to save this place, yet closure has posed problems about where else to care for long- and short-term patients.

These quotations sum up Polly Toynbee's attack on the policy of closing mental hospitals without providing alternative accommodation. An under-secretary at the Ministry of Health, Mr Stephen Dorrell, took part:

> We have to ensure that there are proper support arrangements within the community, so that those who need support as a result of mental illness have it delivered to them in an ordered way, rather than having to report to casualty departments. We also have to ensure that there are proper systems to ensure that if people fall out of community care for whatever reason, or they reject what is available, or the system loses touch with them, then there is what I call a ladder back into the proper systems of care.

Mr Dorrell's sentiments were impeccable, but no one, as far as I am aware, believes they are represented by any action in the real world.

Polly Toynbee was not only concerned with mentally disturbed offenders, but the mentally ill generally. She provides some striking examples drawn from the offender category. The following dialogue is typical of a number of human cases provided by her:

Toynbee: 'Animal', the Electric Gypsy, as he calls himself, has waited five months to be transferred from Brixton Prison to a psychiatric ward here at London's University College Hospital. Why did they send you here?

Animal: Well, because, like it is claimed, I have a psychiatric disorder. I get a bit violent sometimes when I am upset.

Toynbee: What were you accused of?

Animal: The original charge was burglary, but I was accused also of using a pickaxe, a sledgehammer and a crowbar to damage somebody with intent to kill.

Toynbee: How much harm did you do them?

Animal: Their kneecaps, their elbows, their hand, broke their nose and their teeth, their eye, their head – just didn't like them.

Toynbee: 'Animal' needs treatment, but someone also has to leave hospital today to make room for him. The mentally ill in prison, on the streets and alone in the community are competing for fewer and fewer hospital beds.

Those who like myself criticize the failure to provide proper treatment for mentally disordered offenders are making two main complaints: first, that there is not the provision that there should be for them in prison, in special or mental hospitals, or in the community; second, that even with existing facilities they could be handled with much more enlightenment. The first submission is irresistible. The second hardly less so.

V   Sex Offenders in Prison

In the autumn of 1991, I visited individual sex offenders in Wandsworth and Chelmsford prisons. The prisoner in Wandsworth had been convicted of offences against boys, the prisoner in Chelmsford against his granddaughter; both insisted on their innocence. The prisoner in Wandsworth had an excellent record as a schoolmaster. He was a naturist and had for a number of years photographed naked boys in his house but, he maintained, at all times innocently. The prisoner in Chelmsford, a respected foreman within the London transport system, assured me that his wife had been present throughout the incident which had got him into trouble.

I also visited the Gracewell Clinic in Birmingham and (not for the first time) Grendon, then Littlehey, Whatton and Belmarsh prisons, for the first time. I had visited Maidstone many times but on this occasion I concentrated on sex offenders. The same is true of Wakefield. I enjoyed fruitful discussions in all these places. Again and again it was brought home to me that to help sex offenders one has got to overcome the denial factor, in other words their insistence on their innocence. How this is to be done without undue pressure on the inmate remains a delicate question. Given sufficient resources, however, I am convinced that much can be accomplished in helping sex offenders to return to society with some degree of confidence that they will not offend again.

This is all the more necessary when we look at the excellent pamphlet, *Sex Offenders in Prison*, published by the Prison Reform Trust in 1990. It begins in this way: 'During the past few years the number of sex offenders in our gaols has grown rapidly. In 1981, there were in prison 1,110 people who had been convicted of sex offences; by 1988 there were 2,692. Sex offenders now account for

7 per cent of the total sentenced prison population; in 1981 the figure was only 4 per cent.' It continues: 'First . . . the issue of Rule 43. The rise in the number of sex offenders in prison has led to a quadrupling of the number of prisoners on Rule 43, necessitating the provision of parallel but separate régimes for a growing proportion of the prison population . . .' It is pointed out that the Rule 43 prisoners are mainly but not entirely sex offenders.

Rule 43 prisoners have a much more restricted life than other prisoners, which is saying a good deal. On the other hand there were 660 prisoners in vulnerable prisoner units (VPUs) who are not included in these figures and for whom a more normal régime is in theory provided. The Prison Reform Trust argue convincingly that the huge increase in the number of sex offenders in prison is brought about by increased sexual crime, more severe sentencing policy and more restrictions in the granting of parole.

Recently, the Home Office has come forward with what can fairly be claimed to be a new approach to the whole question of sex offenders in prison. There is no provision for increased resources, however, and it is difficult therefore to believe that at the moment this programme is more than pie in the sky, but pie in the sky is a lot better than pie nowhere if we can persuade ourselves that in the foreseeable future it is going to descend to earth.

Let me quote two paragraphs from the Government's proposals. They intend to introduce:

1. A core programme, which does not require significant resources, [to] tackle offenders' distorted beliefs about relationships, enhance their awareness of the effect of sexual offences on the victim, and seek to get inmates to take responsibility for, and face up to, the consequences of their own offending behaviour. The programme will also get inmates to develop relapse prevention strategies, identifying the nature of their offence cycles and how high risk situations can be avoided.
2. An extended programme, for those who represent the greatest risk, [to] be run at establishments with appropriate specialist resources. This will, in addition, tackle problems of deviant arousal, interpersonal relationships, communication skills, anger and stress management, substance abuse, etc.

The second proposal seems at first sight to be non-controversial. It fits in with the demand made by so many authorities – the illustrious Professor West, for example – for 'specialist units', and it appears to draw a good deal of inspiration from the Gracewell Clinic in Birmingham run by Ray Wyre.

Grendon Prison obviously comes in here. I have visited Grendon many times since it was founded in 1963, but I had not studied the special question of sex offenders there until my visit in autumn 1991. I was told that there were 188 prisoners, of whom 60 or so were sex offenders. Of the latter, 37 were in a special wing, though they mixed freely with the other prisoners at work. I spent an hour with a group of the sex offenders in this special wing. They told me that they had the advantage of a newly introduced psycho-educational treatment. This was in addition to the forms of therapy long maintained in the prison with much emphasis placed on the group discussions.

These discussions, it would appear (and I have sat in on one in the past), are free-ranging and carried out by the prisoners themselves, though a prison officer is usually present. The psycho-educational treatment is much more structured and under professional guidance. The prisoners were well satisfied with the help they were getting and the new understanding of themselves they were acquiring. The chairman of the group, however, serving nine years for seducing his fifteen-year-old daughter, told me that he thought that he had still some way to go before his treatment was complete. He had been at Grendon for two years and seemed to think that another year was necessary.

As with other groups I have visited, I did not expect a definitive answer to the question, 'Why did you do it?' I would find it just as difficult if somebody said to me, 'Why did you become a politician?' But several of the prisoners at Grendon told me that sex, although of course a factor, was not the ultimate motivation. In Whatton Prison, there had been something of a consensus that the desire for power had been strongly at work. In Grendon, the emphasis was laid on the desire to be loved. I am bound to add that one prisoner, who had tried to rape his mother, said that his motivation was anger. He had been abused as a boy by his father, now dead, and he was taking it out on her. All, as I say, felt that they were being assisted by the régime towards a state of mind which would mean that (hopefully) they would not offend again. When I suggested to the governor that the psycho-educational régime would make the treatment more expensive, he told me that this was not so. The professionals concerned were always working in or with the prison.

The good news from Grendon is that the Home Secretary, after a recent visit, had apparently promised that there will be a second Grendon. This has been demanded for several years by penal reformers. The governor at the time of my visit, Mr Selvey, was about to retire after a career of true distinction in the prison service. He felt that the Home Secretary's announcement was a real vindication of the Grendon principles. In my view the Home Office in dealing with sex offenders, as with other offenders, have much to learn from Grendon. Personally, I have always thought that there ought to be several Grendons where the régime can honestly be described as therapeutic. It must be recognized, however, that all who go to Grendon are volunteers, ready to play their part in a system of personal disclosure that would not appeal to many, perhaps most people, offenders or otherwise.

Can we expect the government to set up therapeutic units on the lines of either Gracewell or Grendon? Even if unlimited resources were available, neither would provide an exact model. In the real world such forms of treatment are likely to be more expensive than what any government is likely to think affordable. Nevertheless, they provide a challenge. I have an uneasy suspicion that the Home Office at the moment do not envisage any full-time therapeutic units. Let us hope that they can be persuaded to raise their sights.

Any form of specialist treatment is much more expensive than the newly announced core programme which will apply to the great majority of sex offenders – though the term 'majority' must give us pause. The Home Office proposals (since modified) would apply initially only to those serving more than four years. This requirement will exclude a percentage of the 2,000-odd sex offenders in the system. I gather that the percentage is not as large as one might suppose. It is perhaps less than one-third.

However, and here there is a good deal of difference of opinion among those directly concerned, the Home Office confine their new proposals to those who willingly accept treatment. A prison governor recently told me that most sex offenders begin by rejecting treatment but can be persuaded to undergo it. The sanction which appears to be most effective is that they know that if they do not accept treatment, they will be moved to a less agreeable régime. The governor of Belmarsh Prison told me he had little difficulty when in Wormwood Scrubs in persuading sex offenders to accept treatment. It had been possible there to threaten them with removal to a less congenial prison such as Wandsworth. He had not got that option at Belmarsh but expected to be left with only a few prisoners who would require segregation.

What of the core programme itself? It is being operated in Littlehey Prison, which I visited and where I learnt a great deal. The Chief Inspector of Prisons has given Littlehey a fine bill of health, although he does not pronounce on the advisability of prison officers with very limited training performing therapeutic tasks. The Prison Reform Trust, in *Sex Offenders in Prison*, picked out Littlehey as pioneering the integration of sex offenders with other prisoners, but I remain sceptical about the amount of worthwhile therapy that can be provided by prison officers after a very short training. They receive much less training than do nursing officers and substantially less than the two years received by probation officers, such as those employed at Gracewell. I have no wish to be derogatory about prison officers *per se*, but it is all a question of resources (always limited), and so it will be with other prisons who introduce the new core programme.

This brings us to the question of the integration of sex offenders with other prisoners. Most sex offenders, the so-called nonces, are treated appallingly in prison at the present time. The two sex offenders I visited in Chelmsford and Wandsworth were quite certain that they would be seriously maltreated if they joined the main prison population. We must therefore give careful attention to the pioneering work at Littlehey. Out of 550 prisoners, some 250 are sex offenders, of whom somewhat less than half are in A Wing.

The sex offenders in A Wing sleep in this separate wing but they mix with the rest of the prison population for work and education and so on. But the majority of the sex offenders in Littlehey share the full life of the prison. If anyone asks me whether this works well, I reply that it seems to provide a better life for sex offenders than is provided for them elsewhere. I was told that through group therapy they obtain a feeling of safety within their own circle, and through mixing with the other prisoners they obtain the additional feeling of safety by acceptance in the 'general public'. This double feeling of safety is highly beneficial to therapy.

I was able to talk to a group of sex offenders in Littlehey. I never expect to find a group of prisoners who are satisfied with a prison – I am sure I would not be if I were a prisoner – and I hesitate therefore to base myself too closely on what they told me. The prevailing view, however, seemed to be that they would be better off if A Wing were not a separate entity. They felt that they would enjoy more respect from staff and other inmates if they were not so clearly identified. It may be that in a prison like Littlehey, where almost half the prisoners are sex offenders, there would be reasonable safety in such an arrangement.

A week after my visit to Littlehey, I was able to visit Whatton Prison. The prisoners at Whatton are nearly all sex offenders. I spent an hour there, also, with a group and found that they much preferred the total safety of Whatton to being in a mixed prison, even one as enlightened as Littlehey. I raised with the staff the question of the transition from this 'total safety' to the harsh world outside. Would it be best to move an inmate to an ordinary prison – Littlehey, for example – on the way to freedom? The staff did not think so. They saw the answer in arrangements for prisoners to work outside before they finally left prison.

Leaving integration for the moment and reverting to treatment, I was impressed by the multi-disciplinary approach of Whatton. The group I sat with were undergoing a course arranged by two probation officers and two prison officers. This seemed to me an advance on Littlehey. I bear in mind, however, that there are 550 prisoners in Littlehey and 160 in Whatton. This may be one more example of the argument that small is beautiful in prisons.

And so to Maidstone. Maidstone has been for many years in my eyes the most enlightened prison since the days of the governors John Vidler and Peter Timms, a tradition maintained by the present governor. There are about 500 prisoners, 100 of them sex offenders segregated in Thanet Wing. But whereas the A Wing prisoners at Littlehey mingle with the other prisoners for work, education and so on, the 100 prisoners in Thanet are completely segregated for good or for ill. The régime for sex offenders at Maidstone is closer to that at Whatton.

I spent about four hours in Maidstone accompanied by the head of the psychological services in that group of prisons and the governor of Thanet Wing, a striking young woman. I also had fruitful meetings with a group of prison officers and two prisoners. The prison officers, like the governor of Thanet Wing, had no doubt about the message they wanted to put across to me: resources and yet again more resources. At the present time there are 26 staff dealing with the 100 prisoners in Thanet Wing. Group therapy has been carried on up until now by only two prison officers plus the psychologist and the probation officer serving on the Wing. If therapy is to be offered on a much wider scale, they will certainly need at the very least four more officers. I questioned the extent to which genuine therapy could be offered by prison officers without any special training. One of the two officers who had run a group told me that he had started the group without any training at all. No one envisaged training of more than 12 weeks at the most. I recognize that the staff on Thanet Wing have the assistance of a probation officer and a psychologist, but a qualified prison nursing officer receives training for about six months. Prison officers playing the part of therapists should receive at least as much. In the absence of more resources, however, the staff on Thanet Wing clearly regarded this as an unreal aspiration.

I asked the governor of Thanet Wing what provision was made under the government's new plans for specialist treatment. She said that all the three stages of the government plan would be conducted in Maidstone: the assessment (where the psychologist would play a big part), the core treatment, and any further specialist provision where again psychologists and, if necessary, psychiatrists would be involved.

The first of the two prisoners I interviewed at Maidstone was serving ten years for conspiracy to bugger. He was an admitted paedophile, an old public schoolboy quite impressive in his way. Before I left he handed me a 23-page document which he had written, beginning 'I intend to write about child love, paedophilia and, because I myself love boys and because this is partly about me, it will concentrate largely on that aspect of paedophilia. First let me make it quite clear that paedophilia means "love of children". It does not include cruelty of any kind or sadism nor abduction nor prostitution nor murder. All too often such values are linked in the public mind and in the tabloid press with paedophilia but they are in no way synonymous.'

He told me that he was innocent of the precise crime of which he was convicted but admitted that he had twice been in trouble before, though this was the first time he was imprisoned. He was primarily attracted by boys of somewhere around the age of 15. They lost their appeal later, though there was a young black man in his wing in his twenties who made some appeal to him. Obviously there was no question of his asking the authorities to treat him or change his nature. When he left prison he planned to go to Spain or Portugal or some other country where the age of consent was 12.

The other prisoner was very different. He had been in prison several times before. He was attracted primarily by boys between the ages of 11 and 15. He felt particularly guilty about this because when he was 11 he had been seduced by his father. Like the other prisoner he had no desire to change his nature but he did realize that his present propensity could be damaging to young boys and he would be happy to fall in love with older men. Interestingly, he was obtaining benefit from his talks with the psychologist. I mentioned this fact to the Wing governor and was told that he was a very rare case. Very few want to undergo that kind of personal treatment.

My final visit was to Wakefield Prison, which is larger than the other prisons discussed here. It contains 700 prisoners as compared with 550 at Littlehey, 500 or more at Maidstone, and only 160 at Whatton. Wakefield contains considerably more sex offenders than any of those: more than 400 against 250 in Littlehey, 150 or so in Whatton and 100 in Maidstone. What is still more striking is the fact that here alone among the prisons I have visited there is total integration, and no Rule 43 or special wing for sex offenders. Is this the ideal? A few prisoners will always require special protection but such people can be transferred away from Wakefield. One benefit is obvious. The prisoners lead a more normal life while in prison than in the other prisons mentioned and in that sense are better prepared for life outside (this is true of only half the Littlehey prisoners). Mr Clark, the Chief Psychologist at Wakefield, discussed all matters at length. He could say with confidence, and this was confirmed by a senior prison officer later, that there is no bullying of the sex offenders. As the prison officer remarked, they were in the majority; there was safety in numbers.

I visited the prison with the original intention of meeting a very unhappy, physically damaged, prisoner who was desperately sad about his conviction for a murder which he claimed that he didn't commit (on appeal the final sentence was manslaughter). His testimony may be regarded with caution but he told me that the horror of prison life was added to by the presence of several hundred sex offenders. The senior prison officer confirmed that that was quite a common reaction among the minority.

I naturally questioned the Chief Psychologist about the treatment provided for sex offenders at Wakefield. He told me that 'groups' had only been started in March 1991 and had been suspended for the moment because of an industrial dispute. Hitherto the treatment had been provided when requested by a team of psychologists which now amounted to eight. I gathered that the period of treatment could not be extensive, but that in the course of their prison sentence perhaps a third of the sex offenders benefited from it.

I pressed him on the question of whether prison officers, virtually untrained, could play an important part in the therapeutic process. Surely he, as a professional man, would agree that treatment should be planned and supervised by professionals like psychologists and probation officers. He agreed up to a point, but surprised me by saying that after two or three years under professional supervision selected prison officers with limited training could run group therapy. I told him that at Maidstone I met a prison officer who had just been 'trained', which turned out to mean that he had received only twelve hours of tuition. The Chief Psychologist did not of course object to my suggestion that training ought to be increased but considered that it was very important that the prison staff should be involved as soon as possible in the therapeutic process.

This led us on to the government's newly announced programme. Like everyone else I have spoken to, the Chief Psychologist was enthusiastic, not so much about the particular features of the programme but about the fact that the government were going to give the treatment of sex offenders an altogether new priority. This would mean in practice that the governor in one of the designated prisons would be expected to make sure that adequate treatment was provided. Like everyone else I have spoken to, the Chief Psychologist cried aloud for more resources to make the programme a success. 'But if you don't get them or don't get them immediately,' I asked, 'what then?' 'No doubt,' he replied, 'staff would have to be transferred from other activities, supervising work for example.'

After visiting several prisons in the autumn of 1991, I am left with a question: if I knew someone who had committed a serious sexual offence, how would I wish him to be placed in prison or another institution? At present he could be placed in a mainstream prison under Rule 43 (Wandsworth or Chelmsford); in a segregated prison wing (Maidstone or in effect Whatton); in a semi-integrated prison (Littlehey or Grendon); or in a fully integrated establishment like Wakefield or Gracewell. At present I doubt whether we can claim with confidence that the sex offender is guaranteed an important element of a just sentence: the institution best able to treat him (or contain him).

I therefore lay the following questions before the government with regard to sex offenders:

• How far do the government propose to bring about integration for the vast majority of prisoners?
• What do they really have in mind when they propose 'specialist treatment'?
• How can the ordinary prison staff be trained to operate the new core programmes effectively?
• What kind of life will be provided in the near future for prisoners who are to remain segregated, perhaps under Rule 43?
• Is the government confident that the 1991 Criminal Justice Bill will provide effective after-care?

Everyone wishes the government's programme to succeed. However, in spite of opening the debate on sex offenders in the House of Lords on 13 November 1991, I have yet to receive positive answers to these questions. I have not met anyone who believes the new programme will succeed without a considerable increase in resources.

VI   Conclusions

In these final pages I shall be mainly concentrating on public policy, in the light of the evidence quoted above and other forms of study. I must dwell, however, for a moment on the theoretical issue which has come home to me more intensely as I delve into this perplexing and largely neglected subject. Are mentally disordered offenders (those who break the law and who suffer some degree of mental abnormality) to be regarded as criminals to be punished, or patients to be treated?

As regards sentencing policy, I have made my views plain in principle in *Punishment and the Punished* (March 1991). Thirty years earlier I had written a small book called *The Idea of Punishment*. On each occasion I distinguish four elements in a just sentence: deterrence, reform of the criminal, prevention (detention to prevent further wrong-doing), and retribution. I have also expressed the hope that reparation would play an ever larger part. In the later book, I recognized that in the earlier one I had neglected the effect of public opinion which was all too likely to interfere with abstract justice.

I considered that punishment, involving some degree of moral condemnation, was based on the idea, essential to a human society, that the vast majority of offenders must be held morally responsible for their actions. The fact that this last assumption is not universally true has led me to write this present book. I will only add that both my previous books attempted to introduce a Christian approach. Punishment intrinsically involves pain, but Christians insist that we should never neglect the possibilities of healing.

From the beginning I have been aware of the ambiguities in the concept of mentally disordered offenders, whether in theory or practice. As I have pointed out, the distinction becomes blurred as soon as one compares the restrictive régime applied to most of the patients in Broadmoor with the relative freedom in open prisons. Again, are we to say that the inmates of the regional secure units are patients, and those of Grendon Prison are criminals? Can we make the distinction between those who are being treated in hospitals entirely from the point of view of the future, and those in the penal system whose treatment is largely conditioned by their past, that is to say, their offence? Should we say that sentencing policy depends on the assumption that those being sentenced are responsible for their actions, and that the fundamental attitude of doctors, including of course psychiatrists, is not concerned with the responsibility or otherwise of their patients? Can we say that sentencing is judgmental, but that the medical approach is essentially non-judgmental?

At this point, Professor Gunn warned me to be careful:

It is not quite right to compare Broadmoor with open prisons because, on the whole, and certainly in a perfect world, people are placed in the level of security which they require, so that a patient who required to be in a maximum security hospital would not be placed by the prison department in an open prison. The real issue seems to be the rationale, the purpose of the two types of organization. The penal system is what it says. As you say – it is there to cause pain. This is a terrible burden for the staff to bear, but that is in fact their job. Hospitals, on the other hand, have an entirely different purpose. Certainly they have to use restraint to prevent patients damaging themselves and others, but their purpose is treatment and the relief of pain.

. . . It is of course true that sometimes patients are placed in deplorable hospital conditions, and sometimes people would be better off if they were in prison, but I do not think the anomalies should divert you from thinking of the two organizations as different. The philosophical basis on which they are founded is bound to have an impact.

How far should the forensic or other psychiatrist be held responsible for the treatment, in the widest sense including the sentence, of someone who has broken the law? Obviously his expert opinion will be invoked to help the court to decide what is best for the abnormal patient. But how far should he be called on to offer expert opinion on the guilt or otherwise of the defendant? Should the psychiatrist confine his evidence to what would be best for the patient, that is the possibilities of reform? In practice, he will often be expected to contribute to the finding of guilty or otherwise, which will bring in decisions about the other elements of deterrence, prevention and retribution in a just sentence. Professor Gunn replied:

> Certainly the psychiatrist will try to decide what is best for his patient. He will usually try to decide what is best for other people in terms of the patient's dangerousness. It is rarely in the interests of a patient to allow him to go on being a threat to others. As for offering expert opinions on 'the moral responsibility or guilt of the defendant', here I have very strong views. This must be left to the court. There can be no such thing as an expert on the moral question. Psychiatrists can give evidence about mental disease and its treatment, but ultimately the judge or jury, or both, must decide about the responsibility and guiltiness.

I realize that the judge or jury must always make the decision about conviction and the sentence. But one has only to turn back to the interviews earlier in this book to find psychiatrists being expected to make recommendations about treatment which in effect may have a crucial influence on the sentence.

Sex offenders, however, who are infinitely varied in their deviations, cut across the ordinary categories. The psychiatrists I have consulted do not appear to regard sex offenders as being ill. They do, however, recognize the need for treatment. Nobody possesses higher authority in this field than Professor West:

> If one is trying to change undesirable sexual behaviour, it means persuading people to change their lifestyle and thus avoid situations which offer temptation. A lot of these things are easier to do outside prison than inside but those offenders who, in the public interest, have got to be imprisoned are entitled to the same treatment as if they were outside.

That would involve the ideal expressed by Judge Tumim, of raising the level of psychiatric care in prisons to that of mental hospitals.

Professor West demands the establishment of special units, attached to prisons and hospitals alike, for dealing with sex offenders – a bold demand, but no one who has looked into these problems is likely to be satisfied with anything less. Are sex offenders to be regarded as criminals or patients, or both? The theoretical problems are not going to go away. They provide a background for the very difficult practical decisions which arise when the disposal of a particular sex offender has to be decided on.

These are indeed deep waters. I will turn with relief to public policy in regard to mentally disordered offenders, and refer again to the letter written by the directors of five relevant institutions to the Home Secretary in July 1990. It was signed by the directors of the National Schizophrenia Fellowship, the Howard League for Penal Reform, MIND, the Prison Reform Trust and NACRO. The first paragraph of the letter summarized the message:

> We have become increasingly concerned about the presence in our prisons of *large* [my italics] numbers of mentally vulnerable individuals. We are therefore writing to urge you to take a number of steps to divert the mentally vulnerable from the criminal justice system, and to improve the standard of care given to those who become mentally disturbed in custody.

This letter was treated by the quality press as of high importance. Some quotations from the directors concerned were sufficiently blunt. Jerry Westall (National Schizophrenia Fellowship):

> Whilst the Home Office is planning to open 24 new prisons by the end of the century, health authorities have plans to close 36 mental hospitals by 1995, with a loss of 12,500 places. The NSF does not wish to see people transferred from hospital care to the penal system because of the lack of appropriate care in the community, but it looks as if this is happening.

Frances Crook (Director of the Howard League for Penal Reform): 'The Howard League is deeply concerned about the number of vulnerable people committing suicide in prison (suicides in prison doubled in the 1980s). Urgent action must be taken so that mentally ill people are cared for properly outside the prison system.' Ian Bynoe (Acting Legal Director of MIND): 'The mentally disturbed suffer significant discrimination from the Health and Social Services and in the criminal justice system.' Stephen Shaw (Director, Prison Reform Trust): 'The detention of mentally ill people is a moral outrage.' The five directors make eight proposals of their own and call attention to another nine made at two recent inquests by the Southwark coroner.

These proposals deserve close consideration. One of them has often been recommended, but that does not make it any the less urgent: 'Immediate steps should be taken towards integration of the prison health service into the National Health Service.' Another proposal could also have far-reaching significance: 'There should be a careful review of Part III of the Mental Health Act of 1983, in order to identify possible legislative improvements to facilitate the diversion of mentally vulnerable offenders from the criminal justice and penal system.'

At this point Professor Gunn comments:

You quote the five directors as agreeing with the simplistic view that because the opening of new prisons is coincident in time with the closing of mental hospitals, somehow these two phenomena must be linked. They will be linked marginally and we have some data (which is still embargoed by the Home Office, but I am struggling to get it released very soon), which indicates that perhaps a thousand people nationally are misplaced in prison and should be in hospital. They would hardly fill up the thirty-six mental hospitals referred to. The inter-relationships between institutions are much more complicated than that, and the severest defect of a lack of inpatient facilities for psychiatric patients is felt by the community, both in people's homes and on the streets. The street-dwellers are of course more likely to get into court, but even then that does not necessarily mean more likely to get into prison.

Professor Gunn and Professor Bluglass are the only professors of forensic psychiatry. Professor Gunn was quoted by the five directors mentioned. He, however, is anxious not to accept exaggerated estimates about the numbers of prisoners who should be transferred to hospital. He considers nevertheless that the true number is significant enough to cause much disquiet. He unfolded to me well-thought-out plans for dealing with the transferred prisoners. To mention only one point, he would increase the 600-odd places in the regional secure units to the 2,000 called for in the Butler Report of 1975. There was general agreement among those who gave evidence to me that action of this kind was called for. Professor Bluglass described his own unit in Birmingham with 600 beds as giving scope for a variety of treatment, and for patients staying up to two years, as compared with the smaller units where the stay averages six months.

Whether or not influenced by the letter quoted from the five directors, the Home Office on 1 September 1990 issued what was officially described as *New Guidelines for Dealing with Mentally Disordered Offenders*. I quote from the press release: 'New guidelines have been issued today for dealing with mentally disordered offenders. These are in the form of a Home Office circular which will be sent to police courts and the Probation Service. It will also be sent to the Department of Health, to health authorities and Social Service departments.'

The circular is largely informative, but the message is clear. It reminds all those concerned *'that prison should be avoided wherever possible'* [my italics]. On the face of it, therefore, the reform organizations and the government are on the same wavelength – they both argue that some of those now in prison should be transferred to medical care outside the prison system. This, however, places new responsibilities on the Department of Health and the NHS, and where is the new money to come from? I assume that no savings are possible on the Home Office vote in view of the lamentable condition of so many of our prisons.

Linked with the issue already indicated is another one that affects all those who are mentally disordered, not just the delinquents. The view is widely held that the closure of mental hospitals has not been compensated for by a corresponding expansion of so-called 'care in the community', and I have no doubt this view is correct. But of all the ambiguities, the concept of care in the community is the most blatant because it can mean so many different things. Professor Wing would like to see care in the community linked to existing mental hospitals; others think of it as involving outpatient care in these hospitals; others see it as provided primarily by local authorities; others again think of it in terms of a mental patient returning to his community and being cared for by his family and neighbours. Be that as it may, 'community care' has not up until now satisfied anybody in practice.

In front of me as I write are two cuttings from the *Guardian*. The first (5 October 1990) is headed 'Lack of Cash Leaves Health Authorities Unable to Help: Mental Health Convict Dumped in Casualty: A Health Authority refused to provide accommodation for a homeless, mentally disordered woman released from prison yesterday because it said it could no longer afford to help such people.'

The second article (9 October 1990) is headed 'Community Care a Farce, Inquest Told'. The first paragraph reads,

The mother of a schizophrenic who killed himself soon after discharge from a psychiatric ward had warned doctors that his condition would worsen if he were sent out into the community. 'I believe that care in the community is just a farce, because it doesn't really exist,' the mother told the St Pancras Coroner's Court. 'What happened was not the hospital's fault. It is a political issue. There just is not enough money to give people adequate care.'

Or let me quote from Marjorie Wallace, in the *Sunday Times* in 1987:

It was a startling idea: to release the mentally ill from asylums and put them back into the mainstream of life, into a caring community. It was a plan born out of compassion, optimism and the discovery of new drugs which controlled some of the most crippling mental diseases. It started 25 years ago and it has been pursued, as a policy, by every government since. At first it worked. But now, 25 years later, the optimism has run dry, the compassion looks threadbare and in too many instances the forces of commercialism are all that is being brought to bear upon the problems of progressively sicker people as they are uprooted. For many people . . . the concept of a caring community amounts to little more than a sick joke.

With news like this, no one can suppose that former mental patients, including mentally disordered offenders, are adequately provided for. So where do we find ourselves now? There is general agreement that a number, admittedly undetermined, of mentally disordered offenders are in prison who should be in hospital. Equally, there is agreement that the facilities provided for former mental patients, offenders and otherwise, are far below what is broadly proclaimed as a standard of community care. There is, moreover, agreement that the two phenomena are interlinked. It seems to be accepted that if adequate provision were made in mental hospitals and the community for mental offenders, hospitals would be much readier to accept such patients than now, and prisons would be readier to transfer them. I shall quote Professor Gunn again:

> You are absolutely right to imply criticism of psychiatrists who do not accept patients with personality disorders because they are 'untreatable'. This is a blatant device in many cases to cover up either the lack of inpatient facilities, or a lack of interest in treating such patients, or both. Admittedly such a group of patients does include a large number of people who would prefer to remain in prison rather than the health system, but there are many who would not and who are denied the opportunity to have inpatient treatment.

So there are two problems, a problem of diagnosis, of identifying the mentally disordered offenders who should be transferred from prison, and the problem of catering for them when they are transferred. The two problems are interlinked.

When we tackle the problem from the angle of a government, we soon find ourselves enmeshed in every kind of administrative tangle: the buck passing from central government to the regions, and from the regions to the districts. It is obvious that a thorough investigation of the health system is required before anybody can say with confidence how much new money is needed from the centre, if mental patients, including mentally disordered offenders, are to be treated humanely. Nobody, however, can doubt that large sums of money from the centre will be required before such aims will be achieved.

Much imagination must be shown if additional funds are to be spent wisely. If the large mental hospitals are to be closed, as ideally they should be, then it is essential that smaller units of an enlightened kind should take their place. I will quote from a letter sent to me by one of the top officials in my own regional health authority:

> In the past, large mental hospitals have provided a degree of secure care to some offender patients. However, with the planned closure of the Victorian asylums, that option is no longer available. The National Health Service has responded by establishing a number of regional secure hospital units, which have been in operation since the mid-1980s. However, this service is only one important element of a total comprehensive service. There is a need for a flexible and diverse National Health Service provision ranging from small localized intensive care wards in each district to longer stay asylums or wards, which provide a safe environment for life for small groups of ten or twelve patients who respond to therapy over a long period of time.

It can also be argued forcefully that the full expensive ritual of a psychiatric hospital is not required for patients mentally disordered and now languishing in prison, who are not thought to be capable of treatment. I know of one man, aged 74, who has been in prison for 50 years, still regarded as a dangerous sex offender. In the future, some provision should be made for him not visible at the moment.

However, we have not even begun to dispose of our topic when we have produced plans for transferring a number of mentally disordered prisoners to hospitals or the community. If it is true that many thousands of prisoners require psychiatric attention to some degree, the great majority of mentally vulnerable prisoners will remain in prison. The case for improving the services provided in prison for the mentally vulnerable therefore becomes overwhelming. A vast improvement in the environment on the lines recommended by Lord Justice Woolf's report of 1990 is a sine qua non of real progress. More specialized psychiatric treatment requires a revolution in medical arrangements. The five directors quoted earlier have called for the complete integration of the PMS with the NHS. So has Professor Bluglass. For my part I have no hesitation in backing them.

There is a limit to what can be achieved in the treatment of mentally disordered offenders by governmental or other collective action. In this respect the mentally ill, whether offenders or otherwise, are no different from, for example, the physically disabled. Again and again throughout this book I have urged the necessity for more generous resources for them. But even with the most generous provision imaginable many acute personal problems will remain outstanding. Their treatment will depend on human wisdom and human compassion and, as I would say, a truly Christian spirit.

Mentally disordered offenders defy easy categories. At one end of the spectrum we have the distressed shoplifter or perpetrator of minor criminal damage who should never be sent to prison and may not need to be sent to hospital either. At the other end, however, we have offenders like Ian Brady, Ronald Kray, and Peter Sutcliffe. All of them committed murder, all were sent to prison before being transferred to hospital, and all are said to be very seriously disordered. Dennis Nilsen, also convicted of murder, is still in prison, although many would call him a psychiatric offender. Unlike the others he would be horrified at the idea of being sent to a special hospital. His self-respect, all that is left to him, would be gravely impaired.

I have talked earlier about the lack of love in the backgrounds of many such cases. Should we seek to apportion blame? On the contrary, the only answer, and it is an answer I insist on, is that we should recognize our Christian duty: our duty to those suffering from these grave handicaps and to those who dedicate their lives to helping them.

Surveying the treatment of mentally disordered offenders in Britain today, I reach certain dogmatic conclusions and submit certain aspirations. I conclude that

- As just stated, the PMS should be integrated with the NHS, and the level of psychiatric care in the prisons should be raised accordingly.
- Provision should be made in the courts for psychiatric assessment on the spot, thus eliminating many delays in the

transfer of mentally disordered prisoners to hospital.

• Courts should be given more power to enforce hospital orders.

• Large mental institutions or special hospitals should be replaced by smaller units. In the meantime they should not be wound down until equivalent provision is available elsewhere.

• The Butler target of 2,000 beds in regional secure units should be achieved in the near future.

• Community care should be no longer, as it so often is today, a farce. It should be pushed ahead with until it lives up to its name.

But that cannot be quite my last word. I described my earlier book *Punishment and the Punished* as a Christian approach to the treatment of those who had broken the law. I would never claim that what I call a Christian approach could only come from professing Christians, although I am bound to believe that it is more likely to come from them. I make the same plea, still more urgently, in the present book.

Setting aside for the moment all questions of public policy and professional expertise, I have referred elsewhere in this book to C Wing, Parkhurst Prison, where some of the most disturbed and disruptive prisoners are living in apparent harmony. I asked the senior nursing officer for the secret. He had no doubt about the answer: 'TLC' – tender loving care. Few of us have not felt the need for tender loving care in our own lives, but no one needs it more than the mentally disordered offender.

Postscript

Two major documents were published near the end of 1991 while this book was approaching completion. The first was an interim report entitled *Review of Health and Social Services for Mentally Disordered Offenders and Others Requiring Similar Services*. The review Committee had been established by the Department of Health and Home Office Ministers on 30 November 1990. It is known as the Review of Services for Mentally Abnormal Offenders and is chaired by Dr John Reed, Senior Principal Medical Officer, Department of Health. The second document was called *Mentally Disordered Prisoners*, a report by Professor John Gunn, Dr Tony Maden, and Dr Mark Swinton. The report was commissioned and published by the Home Office. Professor Bluglass and Professor Gunn were (no doubt influential) members of the first Committee. He and Professor Gunn gave invaluable evidence to my own inquiry. The conclusions of these two most important reports will come as no surprise to readers of the foregoing pages. The membership of Dr Reed's Committee ranged far and wide. It included two representatives of the Metropolitan Police and a prison governor. It is fair to say, however, that the approach by and large treats mentally disordered offenders as patients. Nothing is said about punishment. We are told that the report is 'an overview by the Steering Committee of the reports submitted by its community, hospital and prison advisory groups'. We are told that a second tranche of groups will consider finance, staffing and training and research.

'The Government's long-standing policy,' says the report, 'has been that mentally disordered offenders needing care and treatment should receive it from the health and personal social services rather than in custodial care'. The Committee support that policy while making clear that practice 'all too often falls a long way short of what is desirable'. One is bound to notice an ambiguity here and elsewhere in the report. In the first place the transfer of a number of mentally disordered offenders to special hospitals would hardly remove them from what a layman would call custody. In the second place the report goes on to acknowledge that a large number of mentally disordered prisoners will inevitably remain in 'custody' whatever reforms are introduced. The report quotes research by Professor Gunn as suggesting that between 756 and 1,371 sentenced prisoners may currently require transfer to hospital for psychiatric treatment. There are others on remand who might have been diverted before or when they came to court. However, there will still be prisoners who develop or have continuing mental health care needs while in prison. For example, Gunn found that 38 percent of his sample of adult male prisoners had a psychiatric diagnosis, but that the majority did not fulfil the criteria for transfer to hospital under the Mental Health Act. The report agrees to proposals that a full mental health care service should be obtained by contract from the National Health Service initially for remand prisoners. This step, while beneficial, is in my view a poor second to a transfer of the Prison Medical Service to the National Health Service.

It will also come as no surprise that there should be a major expansion of the regional secure units as pressed so strongly by Professor Gunn. At least 1,500 places will be needed nationally, compared with the present 635. Other vital reforms in the system are suggested, some of them, it may well be, stemming from Professor Bluglass. 'In particular there should be more secure provision for people with special needs.'

What is said about special hospitals confirms evidence given to me. 'There are estimated to be some 400 special hospital patients who may not require that level of security. A similar number of sentenced prisoners may need special hospital care.'

The report says bluntly what is indeed obvious. 'Many of the recommendations emerging from the review have resource implications.' In the meantime, they call for much more effective collaboration between the various agencies.

The report of Professor Gunn, Dr Maden and Dr Swinton will remain a treasure trove of information about mentally disordered prisoners for many years. No serious student of these matters can fail to read and digest it thoroughly. In view, however, of the evidence given to me by Professor Gunn and the interim report of the Reed Committee of which he was a prominent member, I will confine myself here to quoting his summarized recommendations.

- Adequate health services in prison.
- Adequate training for all prison staff. Standards of health care in prisons should be the same as those provided by the NHS.
- A prison health service must develop clear policies on the management of psychiatric problems.
- There is a need for clarification of the roles of the prison service in managing mental disorder. Professor Gunn considers that the present policy of making 'staff aware of the cost of treating patients' has serious implications for mentally disordered prisoners. 'The mentally disordered offender may fall uncomfortably between the health and prison systems.' As the health service restricts the service it provides, the prison service could easily be left to make up the shortfall. Professor Gunn and his colleagues conclude: 'As medical care is to be organized increasingly according to the principle of money following the patient, consideration should be given to the possibility of the prison service charging health districts/regions for psychiatric care which they deliver to the district/region's patients. The high level of these charges would reflect the difficulty of providing psychiatric care in prison and provide an incentive for the district/region to provide it elsewhere.'

The key sentence is, 'The mentally disordered prisoner may fall uncomfortably between the health and prison systems.' I cannot myself believe that this problem will be solved merely by more enlightened ministers or ministerial committees or for that matter by more intelligent co-operation between officials. Legislation will be needed. It may take various forms, but at the least it should be made easier to insist that mentally disordered prisoners should be transferred to special or other mental hospitals, as the need arises.

Index

Page numbers in **bold** type refer to principal interviews, ideas and accounts